THE
FIELD&STREAM
Baits and Rigs
Handbook

The *Field & Stream* Fishing and Hunting Library

FISHING

The Field & Stream *Baits and Rigs Handbook* by C. Boyd Pfeiffer

The Field & Stream *Bass Fishing Handbook* by Mark Sosin and Bill Dance

The Field & Stream *Fish Finding Handbook* by Leonard M. Wright Jr.

The Field & Stream *Fishing Knots Handbook* by Peter Owen

The Field & Stream *Fly Fishing Handbook* by Leonard M. Wright Jr.

The Field & Stream *Tackle Care and Repair Handbook* by C. Boyd Pfeiffer

FORTHCOMING TITLES

HUNTING

The Field & Stream *Bow Hunting Handbook* by Bob Robb

The Field & Stream *Deer Hunting Handbook* by Jerome B. Robinson

The Field & Stream *Firearms Safety Handbook* by Doug Painter

The Field & Stream *Shooting Sports Handbook* by Thomas McIntyre

The Field & Stream *Turkey Hunting Handbook* by Philip Bourjaily

The Field & Stream *Upland Bird Hunting Handbook* by Bill Tarrant

THE
FIELD&STREAM
Baits and Rigs
Handbook

C. Boyd Pfeiffer

Illustrations by Cliff Shelby

THE LYONS PRESS

*To the memory of my dear wife, Jackie, who always
was and always will be the inspiration for everything
that I have done, everything I do, and everything
that I might accomplish.*

Copyright © 1999 by C. Boyd Pfeiffer

Printed in the United States of America

10 9 8 7 6 5 4 3 2 1

Library of Congress Cataloging-in-Publication Data

Pfeiffer, C. Boyd.
    The field & stream baits and rigs handbook / C. Boyd Pfeiffer.
        p.   cm.—(The field & stream fishing and hunting library)
    Includes bibliographical references (p. 105) and index.
    ISBN 1-55821-883-1
    1. Bait.   2. Fishing rigs.   I. Title.   II. Title: Field and stream
    baits and rigs handbook.   III. Series.
    SH448.P45   1999
    799.1—dc21   98-52123
                                                                                CIP

Contents

Acknowledgments

This book is built upon the writings, experiences, and teachings of many others over many years. It answers the questions that a favorite uncle asked me about a snelled hook when I was six or seven. He wanted to know how to use it, and I had no idea—nor did anyone else in our family.

Too many times the pleasure of fishing is spoiled by a lack of knowledge—early or late in life—about how to rig a bait or lure, the best knot to use, how to prepare the best bait for a particular fish, or which sinker or hook to use. This little book is meant to answer those questions.

I appreciate very much the help of Cliff Shelby, a good friend and fine artist who, except where otherwise credited, drew the fine illustrations for this book. I also appreciate the help, fine editing, and patience of the staff at The Lyons Press.

THE
FIELD&
STREAM
Baits and Rigs
Handbook

Introduction

T HE FIELD & STREAM *Baits and Rigs Handbook* is designed to be used in the field, but it will serve you best if you pay a little attention to it *before* you go fishing. At home you will be under less pressure to learn a new knot or understand a different bait rig— and you won't waste precious fishing time.

Unlike a novel, there is no plot and no specific order to the information. You can start anywhere that you find useful. I have also included a bibliography, to guide you to other books on the subject.

I sincerely hope this small volume will help you land a fish or two that you might otherwise have missed.

—C. BOYD PFEIFFER

Hooks, Sinkers, Floats, Lines, Leaders, and Terminal Tackle

HOOKS

Hooks have been around in the form that we know them today for about 6,000 years. But while they were once crude and made of bone, brass, or bronze, today there are thousands of different styles, each in dozens of sizes, finishes, colors, wire thicknesses, and shank lengths.

Hooks are available in single point, double point, and triple point (treble hooks) for all types of lure and bait fishing. Lure hooks usually have regular-length shanks, straight eyes (not turned up or down), rounded bends, and straight or curved points. These hooks come in the standard single-point, double-point, or treble-hook format. Single hooks are usually used on spoons, spinnerbaits, buzzbaits, jigs, and with soft-plastic worms; double hooks are found on some spoons; treble hooks are used on spinners, topwater plugs, and crankbaits.

Bait hooks can be long shank (for hooking minnows and other lengthy baits), or short shank (for fish eggs, corn kernels, or cheese chunks). Many have turned-up or turned-down eyes to make it easy to snell them—to wrap the line around the shank in order to "tie" the hook to the line, creating a built-in leader. Both wire (for toothy fish) and monofilament (for most fishing) are used for snells, although mono is much easier to tie. Snelling keeps the mono in a straight line with the hook shank and is much preferred for bait fishing since the line attachment is on the hook, rather than at the end, and thus often

3

hidden in the bait. Snelled hooks are sold, but you can easily make your own. Note that only hooks with turned-up or turned-down eyes can be properly snelled.

Always use a hook of the correct size for the fish you are after. Hook size does not always match fish size: Some large fish have big mouths and take big baits, while others have small mouths and can only take small baits. Almost every lure comes rigged with a hook of the size and design best for the fish size and species for which the lure is intended.

Hook sizes are numbered, with size 1 being suitable for bass, sea bass, flounder, carp, catfish, and similar fish in the 1- to 3-pound range. Smaller hooks have larger numbers and are usually only available in even sizes. Hooks range down to about size 12 to 14 for many bait models, and down to such small sizes as 20 to 28 for midge flies. Larger hooks use a "/O" designation (said to indicate "ocean," although they are also used in fresh water). Thus, sizes ranging from 1/O to 10/O are increasingly larger. These hooks are usually available in both even and odd number.

Hooks generally consist of an eye (to which the line is tied), shank, bend, point, and barb. The eye can be straight, turned up, or turned down. Straight eyes are essential for attaching to lures, rigs, or split rings. A turned-up or turned-down eye is best for bait fishing.

The shank length will vary with the type of hook: Long-shank hooks are ideal for fish that take minnows (trout in fresh water, flounder in salt water), and for toothy fish (pike in fresh water, bluefish in salt water). Special baitholder hooks are available with barbs on the shank to keep baits from sliding off. Treble bait hooks also have a spring around the shank; this helps hold on prepared baits such as doughballs for carp fishing.

The type of bend in a hook also varies, with some bends round, others angled, and some very large to provide the maximum gap. Hooks with a large gap are best for bulky baits or soft-plastic lures; a sufficient gap remains through the bait or lure to hook a fish. Kirbed, or offset, hooks—bent to one side—are designed for bait, since they tend to catch in the fish's mouth and make hooking easier.

Worm hooks with a wire guard are useful when you are fishing in areas with weeds or other underwater obstructions. The small wire attached to the hook acts as a deflector and keeps the line from getting snagged. At the same time, it is sensitive enough to bend out of the way when a fish strikes the hook.

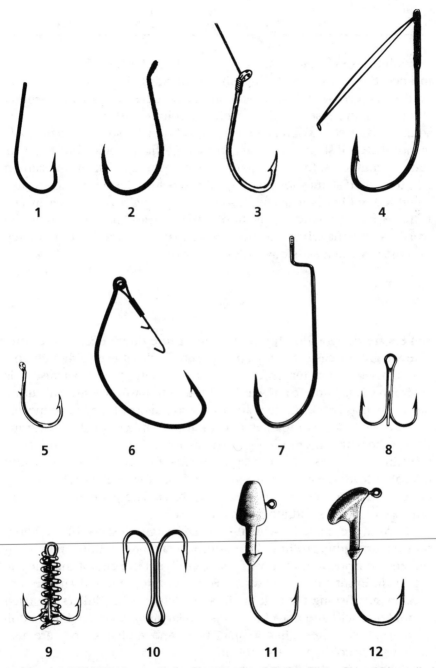

1—Mustad 34043BLN, size 2; 2—Daiichi, size 3/0; 3—Eagle Claw 031 snelled hook, size 1; 4—Gamakatsu 65114 worm hook, size 4/0; 5—Eagle Claw 038 baitholder hook, size 4; 6—Mustad 37752BLN hook, size 4/0; 7—Gamakatsu 07113 worm hook, size 3/0; 8—VMC round treble hook, size 6; 9—Eagle Claw 374SB soft-bait hook, size 6; 10—VMC 9508 double hook, size 2; 11—Owner Ultrahead jig hook 5147; 12—Owner Ultrahead jig hook 5144.

Points also vary, with most being long and having a barb designed to keep the fish from coming off the hook. Barbless hooks are also available; these work just as well but make it easier to remove a hook from the fish (essential for catch-and-release fishing). Conversely, some hooks have two in-line barbs as additional insurance against losing a fish. Hook shanks also vary, from long-shank hooks for long baits such as minnows, to short shanks for burying a hook into a salmon egg, to barbed shanks for holding baits and soft plastics. Some are also weighted, which is a useful feature for getting a bait down in fast water. Special plastic worm hooks bend near the eye so that the worm is straight when the hook is run through the head and back into the body in a classic weedless Texas rig.

SINKERS

Sinkers are designed both to get a bait or lure down deep and to provide weight for casting. They are typically made of lead, although government legislation may soon limit or eliminate its use because it is environmentally unsafe and has been found to harm wildlife. Substitute metals such as brass, tin, steel, and tungsten are now being introduced.

Several tackle companies already make sinkers of these alternatives; others use them as replacement materials in traditional lead-head lures such as spinners, spinnerbaits, buzzbaits, and jigs. These nontoxic lead substitutes are also available for anglers who like to mold their own sinkers and leadhead lures. The general shape and purpose of sinkers and lures remain the same.

Sinkers are made in several different categories: bottom holding, bottom dragging, trolling, lure addition, and drift. Bottom-holding sinkers are made in a variety of shapes to keep the end of the line stable in different bodies of water. For example, pyramid sinkers are used in surf fishing for holding in sand, while bank sinkers are used to hold on rocks and gravel bottoms. Dollar sinkers (shaped like a dollar coin), bell sinkers (like a small bell), and similar shapes are also designed for holding on the bottom.

Sinkers used for drifting are designed to drag along the bottom. These include "walking"-type sinkers, those made with a weight molded on the end of a long wire, and those with a lead rod placed in rubber tubing.

Casting sinkers, which are used with baits and lures, have a small

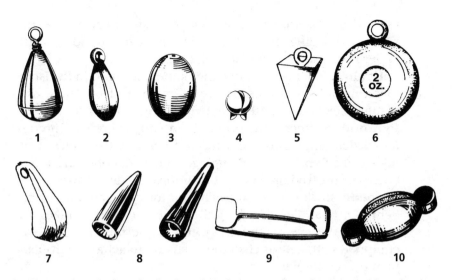

1—bass-casting sinker; **2**—bank sinker; **3**—egg sinker; **4**—removable split shot; **5**—pyramid sinker; **6**—disc, or dollar, sinker; **7**—walking sinker; **8**—worm slip sinker; **9**—pinch-on sinker; **10**—rubber-grip sinker. *Illustrations courtesy of Bullet Weights.*

wire eye that makes them easy to tie onto the end of a line. They are designed to provide casting weight and are also ideal when you are using a float to hold baited hooks below the water. Other sinkers for float rigs include pinch-on (with "ears" at each end to hold the line), rubber grip (with a rubber core that is twisted to hold the sinker on the line), and split shot (pinched tight onto the line with pliers).

Special sinkers are also made to allow fish to run with a bait without dragging the sinker. Egg sinkers and some walking sinkers have this feature, although almost any sinker can be adapted for it with special rigging.

Here are some of the common sinker styles and a brief description of their uses.

- **Bass, bass-casting, or dipsy sinker:** A basic sinker, used to hold on the bottom or as a weight in a float rig. Often made with eyes that allow easy snap-on attachment and removal.
- **Bank sinker:** Has an eye molded in place, used for holding on rocky bottoms.
- **Egg sinker:** Features a hole through the center of the egg for

line to run. Useful when you want a fish to run with a bait without dragging the sinker, as in carp fishing and surf fishfinder rigs. Also used as a general trolling sinker.

- **Split shot:** Pinches onto the line. Sometimes used in fly fishing to get nymphs, wet flies, or streamers down deep. Often used in multiples to distribute weight and control sink rate.
- **Pyramid sinker:** Used primarily in surf fishing. Its three or four sides work into the sand and prevent the sinker from rolling or the baits from dragging. Some variations have longer bodies or protruding wires for additional holding power.
- **Torpedo sinker:** Used in trolling, or for dragging lures or bait behind a boat. The line is tied to one eye of the sinker; the leader, to the eye on the other end of the torpedo. Some are equipped with a bead chain on each end to act as a swivel and help prevent line twist.
- **Keel sinker:** Trolling sinker shaped like the keel of a sailboat to prevent line twist. The line is tied to one side; a long leader ending with a baited hook or lure, to the other. Some banana-shaped or crescent-shaped sinkers are variations of this style and work the same way to prevent line twist.
- **Cannonball sinker:** Shaped like a cannonball and used for deep fishing and drifting. Sometimes dragged along the bottom.
- **Mushroom sinker:** Shaped like an inverted mushroom to hold on a soft or mucky bottom.
- **Dollar, or disc, sinker:** Shaped like a thick dollar coin, with an eye for tying to the line. These lie flat on the bottom when you are bait fishing.
- **Grapnel sinker:** Comes in many bottom-sinker shapes (often bank or pyramid), all with metal prongs on the side to help hold on a rough bottom.
- **Triangle sinker:** Shaped like an open triangle to hold on sandy bottoms when surf fishing.
- **Longhorn sinker:** Shaped like a Y with an eye in the top center, to prevent pulling or dragging on sandy bottoms. A surf-fishing sinker.
- **Pencil sinker:** Used for drift fishing and often sold in coils. Pencils are cut to the length needed for the current and fishing situation, and slipped into a piece of surgical hose easily attached to the line with a snap.
- **Bait walker:** A long sinker molded onto a wire ending in an

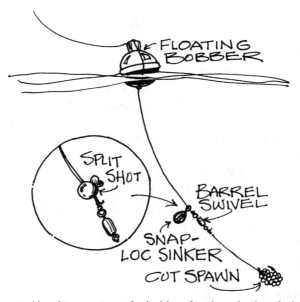

A basic bobber rig like this consists of a bobber fixed to the line, below which is rigged a sinker to hold the bait down and a bait on the hook tied to the end of the line. Different types of slip-on or clamp-on sinkers can be used. *Cliff Shelby.*

eye, and tied to the line to prevent snagging the bait when drift fishing. Skid or sled bait walkers work best on sandy bottoms; those with wire extensions work best on rocky bottoms.

- **Worm weight:** Tapered or cone-shaped weight with a hole through the center to thread onto the line ahead of a worm rig. Provides weight for casting, and helps get a worm deep.
- **Clasp, clinch, or pinch-on weights:** A long-taper sinker (like a cigar) with a lengthwise slot and a tab or ear at each end. The line runs through the slot and often around the sinker a few times to prevent sliding; it is then clinched in place with the two ears.
- **Rubber-grip sinker:** Another long cigarlike tapered sinker, but with a core of firm rubber fitted into the center slot. The line is attached by placing it into the slot and then twisting the rubber tabs at each end to secure it.
- **Diving sinker:** Used in-line (or between the line and a long leader) and equipped with wings or diving planes to help keep it down while trolling.

FLOATS

Sometimes called bobbers, floats are designed to hold baits or lures off the bottom and to signal when a fish strikes or nibbles on them. Floats are available in a wide variety of shapes, styles, and sizes. Round plastic floats are the most common. They easily snap on or off a line, and can be rigged to slide or be fixed to a certain point. Bobber stops are handy additions to these snap-on floats. Several designs are available, but all involve a tiny stop placed on the line; this catches on a bead, which in turn stops the sliding bobber. The stop is small enough to allow casting and to be reeled onto the spool without a problem. During the cast, the bead and bobber slide up the line to stop at this preset point. This allows casting with the bobber already set for very deep fishing.

Different shapes for bobbers include the pear-shaped, barrel-shaped, cigar-shaped, popping, and pencil or quill types. The European bobber styles or float systems are becoming more and more popular. These allow you to use just the right amount of flotation and sensitivity for each purpose. Proper sensitivity is a must for good bait fishing with a float, since the bobber barely floats the weight and strikes are then easier to detect. Most floats are also brightly colored to help you spot them on the water.

Floats attach to the line in various ways. Some have nothing more than a line hole through the center, with a tapered plug fitted into the hole to hold the float at a specific point on the line. You must thread these onto the line before you tie any rigs, lures, or hooks to the end. Other floats have more elaborate snaps and swivels.

Most floats are designed to sit on the surface and hold a suspended hook and sinker above the bottom. Some are designed to work below water, such as the hole-through-center floats used next to a hook on bottom rigs. These hold the bait off the bottom or on walking-sinker, drift-bait rigs, or prevent scavenging by crabs and crayfish. In salt water, these are sometimes called fireball rigs.

LINES

Fishing line for most gear (except fly-fishing gear) is made of monofilament nylon; braided Dacron; or the new, extremely thin, braided materials of gel-spun polyethylenes, or Kevlar. Sometimes single-strand or twisted (called braided) wire is used for deep trolling in fresh or salt water. This is usually difficult to handle, however, and tangles unless kept under constant control. Also, regular knots cannot be used with this material; special connections, such as crimping leader sleeves to form loops or haywire twists, are essential.

Buying the best possible line is a good investment. Premium monofilament line is stronger, is more flexible, and has better knot strength than lesser lines. You can use it for almost all types of fishing, because it creates strong knots and in many cases requires no leader—just tie the end of the line directly to the lure, bait rig, or hook.

Dacron line has less stretch and can be used in place of monofilament for trolling, but knots are difficult to hold in Dacron. It is hollow, however, and can be spliced easily using needles.

The new braided lines of Kevlar and Spectra (the best known of the gel-spun polyethylenes) have less stretch and more sensitivity than Dacron, but knots are also more difficult and unreliable. New "thermofusion" lines of twisted gel-spun polyethylene, with a heat treatment that makes them behave more like monofilament, have better knot strength and are less expensive than the braids.

It's important to match your line carefully to your fishing needs. Here are some general tips on line strength.

- For most freshwater fishing, 6- to 15-pound test is recommended—lighter for trout and panfish, heavier for walleye, bass, and catfish.
- For pike, muskies, and heavy freshwater fish, use 15- to 25-pound test.
- Bass fishermen change their lines depending upon fishing conditions; these lines can range from 6- to 17-pound test and even 20- to 40-pound test for "flipping" big fish.
- For freshwater trolling, use 10- to 20-pound test—lighter for panfish trolling, heavier for pike and muskies.
- For most saltwater fishing, use 10- to 20-pound test—lighter for inshore fishing for species up to several pounds, heavier for larger fish or offshore boat fishing.
- For party boat, surf, or bottom saltwater fishing, use 15- to 30-pound test—to handle the size of the fish, but also to get a fish in quickly enough to prevent tangles with other lines on the same boat or beach.

Fly lines differ from all other lines. The weight of the line you use is critical, as are the length and strength of your leaders, which are much lighter than those used in most other types of fishing. Fly lines generally have a 30- to 40-pound-test core, on which a floating or sinking coating is added. The heavy coating is to provide enough weight to cast the fly, and to shape the line's taper to help you turn over the line on your cast. Thus fly casting is really *line* casting, with the fly going along for the ride.

LEADERS

A leader is nothing more than a length of special line (usually monofilament) that connects the fishing line to the lure, hook, or bait rig. It has several functions, depending on the type of tackle you are using and the fish you are catching. In fly fishing, the leader provides a separation between the line and the fly. This keeps the heavier line from "spooking" the fish and helps create a taper at the end of the line, which allows the fly to land gently on the water.

On trolling rigs, a leader allows for the easy attachment of the sinker, which is placed between line and leader. Heavy fishing might require special shock or "bite" leaders to keep fish from biting through the line. Single-strand wire, twisted wire, and heavy monofilament are all used for this purpose. Bite leaders are essential for fish such as pike, pickerel, muskies, bluefish, barracudas, sharks, and other toothed species. Some fish that need bite leaders are very leader shy—mackerel, tuna, or albacore, for example. Use a heavy mono leader for them, although you do risk losing a big fish with this setup.

True shock leaders are sometimes used in surf fishing. These are made of heavier pound test than the line itself, and are long enough that several turns of the leader wrap around the reel spool. Any extreme forces generated by your cast will then be absorbed by the heavy leader, not the weaker line.

Here are some tips on making and using leaders. Do not make them unnecessarily long; for general freshwater and saltwater fishing, they need be only a few feet. And very short leaders are used in fly fishing with sinking lines, to keep the fly down along with the submerged line. Long leaders are best used for trolling, to keep fish from being scared off by the planer or trolling sinker.

Leaders are ideal to use with Dacron or Spectra lines that have low knot strength or require special knots. A leader of monofilament tied to these lines will make lure and hook changing quick and reliable. Remember that some leaders require special knots. For example, when you are attaching a heavy monofilament leader to a line, use a Bimini twist to double the line and then an Albright knot to attach the leader (see chapter 2 for more information on knots). To attach a wire leader to monofilament line, use an Albright knot to a spider hitch or to a Bimini doubled-line twist. For attaching hooks and lures, use a haywire twist in solid wire leader, or a figure-eight knot in braided wire leader.

You can also attach braided wire and nylon-coated braided wire leaders by forming loops using special crimping pliers to crimp leader sleeves in place. Be sure to use the appropriate leader sleeves and crimping pliers for this task. As a general rule, use round sleeves for cup-opposing-point crimping pliers; use double round sleeves for the cup-opposing-cup crimping pliers. Most manufacturers list compatible equipment on sleeve and plier packages.

In fly fishing, successively thinner sections of monofilament are tied together to make a tapered leader. Most fly-fishing leaders start with a butt section of 25- to 30-pound-test mono that is nail-knotted to the end of the fly line, followed by shorter (less than 1 foot) sections of lighter mono, until you reach the tippet.

A good basic rule for fly lines is to use 40 percent of the leader as the butt section, 40 percent as the tapered section, and 20 percent as the tippet to which you tie the fly. Thus, with a 10-foot leader, 4 feet would be a butt section of 25- to 30-pound test; 4 feet would be tapered sections of monofilament of perhaps 20-, 15-, 12-, and 10-pound test; this would be followed by 2 feet of tippet of about 6-pound test. Fly-tackle manufacturers produce a variety of leader and tippet materials that are custom-tapered and weighted for all fishing conditions.

TERMINAL TACKLE

Terminal tackle includes sinkers, hooks, and floats along with many of the smaller items used in fishing, such as swivels, snaps, connectors, and split rings. Swivels are an important but underrated piece of tackle. As a hook or lure gets tossed about in water currents, the fishing line will naturally start to twist. Without a swivel, it can become knotted and tangled. Ball-bearing swivels are more expen-

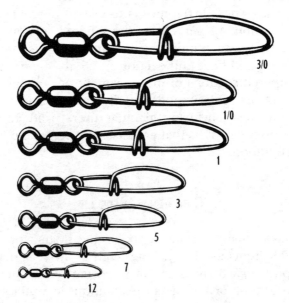

Courtesy of Berkley.

sive than regular ones, but they work much better in preventing these line twists.

Snaps make it easy to change lures, hooks, sinkers, and similar rigs without retying knots. Use small snaps or swivels for fish of up to about 3 pounds, the next-larger size for fish of up to 15 pounds, and increasingly larger sizes for bigger fish.

Your local dealer will likely encourage you to add a snap, split ring, or other connector to any metal lures that lack them. Similarly, spoons are not always supplied with line-tie rings. Since the line-

Courtesy of Berkley.

attachment hole is punched during manufacturing, the sharp edges can gradually wear through the line, resulting in a lost lure or fish.

Finally, when you use a snap or snap swivel with a sinker that has a molded-in lead eye, choose a snap large enough to be closed around the eye. This is one occasion when you might need a larger snap than you would normally require for strength alone.

Knots and Splices

K NOTS ARE USED to tie lines to hooks and lures, to bottom and trolling rigs, to other lines, to make loops in leaders, and to the fishing reel. Splices are used the same way. In addition, there are special attachments that permit no-knot fastening of lines to leaders, hooks, or lures. As we noted in chapter 1, knots in monofilament are easy to make, since the slick nylon pulls up readily, slides smoothly, and has good strength. Other types of line, however, require special treatment.

Before you go fishing, practice tying a few knots. It is far better to learn a few knots that you can use successfully than to learn many knots and be less sure when tying them. Make sure that you tie knots *exactly* as shown to prevent slippage or weakness. And remember that most knots intended for tying line to a hook or lure can also be used to tie to sinkers, and to any snap, swivel, bottom, or trolling rig. Here are a few tips for all lines and connections.

Always pull knots up tight; slippage is one of the main reasons that knots come undone or break. One way to prevent slippage is to seal a knot after tying with one of the fast-drying superglues known as cyano-acrylates. Another useful tip is to wet the knot with saliva to help lubricate it as you pull it tight.

Remember to leave enough tag end on the line. All knots should then be trimmed with scissors or clippers to within about 1/16 inch. Do *not* use a cigarette lighter or flame to form a molten ball on the end, since the heat will weaken the knot. It's also potentially dangerous.

Keep the number of knots in any rig or fishing system to a minimum; any knot is a potential weak spot. If you are ever in doubt about a knot, cut it off and retie it. At the same time, knots were developed for special tasks, so it follows that there is always a right knot for the job. For example, use special knots such as the three-turn Palomar for the new braided lines of Spectra or Kevlar to increase their strength.

If you are attaching a line to a rig, hook, or lure that has a large line-tie or eye, consider using the Trilene knot, or a double-turn Palomar or similar knot. A clinch knot or improved clinch knot tends to slip or open up when tied to large-diameter wire. If you are tying to a split ring, turn it so that you are on the double-wire area, not the small single-wire area. The butt ends of the doubled wire can wear and abrade the knot.

If you are tying sinkers or rigs to be used on the bottom in sandy areas, protect the knot from abrasion by using a bead next to it. This will prevent sand from getting in and around the knot if you are using an egg sinker. Another option is to run rubber tubing over the knot.

One of the first knots you need to tie is the one connecting your line to your fishing reel. Here are some proven knots for this purpose.

- **Casting reels:** Run the line through the levelwind mechanism, then loop the line once or twice around the spool arbor and tie an overhand knot in the end around the standing line. Pull up carefully and trim any excess tag end. With the line coming off the turning line spool, maintain constant tension as you spool the line on the casting reel to within about ⅛ inch of the rim.
- **Fly reels:** You should use what is known as an arbor knot. Pass the line around the reel arbor, then tie an overhand knot around the standing line. Tie a second overhand knot in the tag end, pull tight, and cut off excess. Snug down on the arbor.
- **Spinning reels:** Run the line over the line roller and loop it once or twice around the spool arbor. Tie an overhand knot and trim the end as you pull the knot tight. Allow line to spiral off the spool (the spool does not turn) as you run the line through a towel or use another means to create tension while you spool the line. Fill to within ⅛ inch of the lip. Note that if

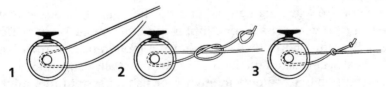

Arbor knot: This is a good knot for attaching line to any reel spool.
   I. Run line around spool arbor.
   2. Tie overhand knot around standing line, then an overhand knot in tag end to prevent slippage.
   3. Pull both knots tight, then pull up to cinch around arbor spool.
Courtesy of Berkley.

the line starts to twist between the spool and the reel, you can turn the spool over to remove the twist.

- **Spincast reels:** On a spincast reel, run the line through the hole in the nose cone first and tie a loop around the spool as above. Trim the end of the knot. Spool under tension, as with a spinning reel. Remove the nose cone frequently to check on the amount of line; too much will make casting difficult with this type of reel.

There are hundreds of knots and knot variations for fishing. Here are a few of the more popular and useful ones, starting with the uni-knot system.

- **Uni-knot system:** This is not just one knot, but a series of knots developed by outdoor writer Vic Dunaway that use the same basic tying methods. The basis for the knot is an overhand loop in the line, with the tag end then wrapped several times around both lines. It is easy to tie for many purposes and has

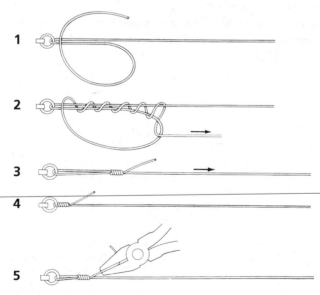

Uni-knot to hook
  1. Run line through eye of hook, and fold over as shown.
  2. Make six turns around doubled line and through circle of line.
  3. Pull line to tighten.
  4. Continue pulling and trim knot.
  5. To make a loop, pull back on the tag end before trimming knot.
Courtesy of Stren.

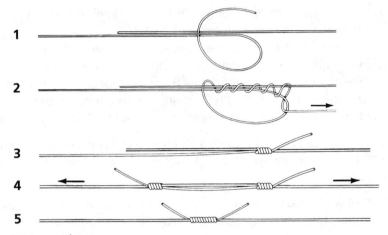

Line-joining uni-knot
1. Overlap two lines and fold back one to make circle crossing in center of two lines.
2. Make several turns of uni-knot around two lines and through circle.
3. Pull tag end tight around line.
4. Make second identical knot around other line and snug tight.
5. Pull two lines to snug knots against each other and trim.

Courtesy of Stren.

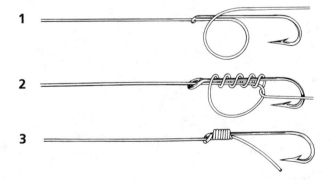

Uni-knot snell
1. Thread line through hook eye and make circle of line around hook.
2. Make several or more turns of line around loop and hook shank and through circle.
3. Tighten by simultaneously pulling line, tag end, and hook shank.

Courtesy of Stren.

high knot strength. Using this technique, it is possible to snell a hook, tie a line to a hook or lure, or join two lines together. Here are just some of the possibilities.

A wide variety of knots can be used to attach the fishing line to a hook or lure. Here are some of the favorites.

- **Improved clinch knot:** An easy knot to tie, with high strength (about 95 percent), and one that does not require making any loops of line back around the hook or lure. Best for monofilament but not recommended for wire or braided lines.

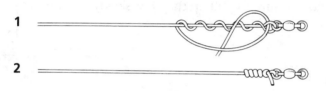

Improved clinch knot
1. Pass line through eye of hook or lure, then wrap around standing line five times and pass through loop formed in line (not hook eye), then back through large loop in line.
2. Pull knot tight; clip tag end.
Courtesy of Stren.

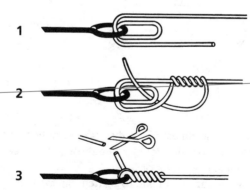

Trilene knot: A good strong knot for attaching line to terminal tackle.
1. Run the end of the eye of the hook or lure twice.
2. Loop tag end around the standing part five or six times and thread end (tag end) back through the eye and line coils as shown.
3. Pull tight slowly and trim end to about ¼ inch.
Courtesy of Berkley.

- **Trilene knot:** A variation of the improved clinch knot in which the line is run through the hook eye twice, twisted around the standing line, then run back through the loop formed by the two turns through the hook eye. Recommended for tying to large-diameter line-ties and eyes, and also for light lines when you need maximum knot strength.
- **Palomar knot:** Strong (about 95 percent reliable) and easy to tie. Since a loop goes over the hook or lure, however, it is awkward on big lures or lures with several hooks. The Palomar is the strongest knot for braided lines when you run the double line through the eye three times before you complete the knot. Be sure to pull up the knot slowly and carefully.

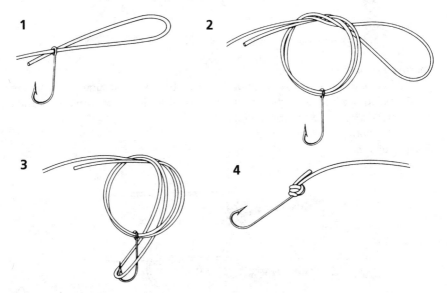

Palomar knot
    1. Double end of line and pass loop through eye of hook or lure.
    2. Make overhand knot with doubled line through hook eye.
    3. Take loop of line over hook or lure.
    4. Pull standing and tag end of line to tighten; clip tag end.
Courtesy of Stren.

- **Homer Rhode loop knot:** Not particularly strong, but easy to tie and reliable when used with a heavy bite or shock leader (the purpose for which it was designed). It provides freedom of movement for a lure or hook.

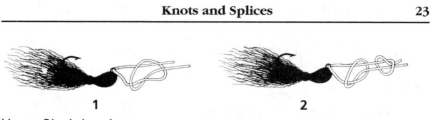

1   **2**

Homer Rhode loop knot
    1. Make overhand knot in fishing line or leader and run tag end through
    hook eye and back through overhand knot.
    2. Tie second overhand knot in tag end around line and pull tight.
Courtesy of Ande.

- **Offshore swivel knot:** Recommended for attaching line to a
  swivel. Usually used after tying a large loop in the line (such as
  a Bimini twist or spider hitch). It is small, tight, and secure in a
  doubled line, and it's often used offshore to rig swivels or snap
  swivels to the end of a line (doubled with a Bimini) before
  attaching long leaders.

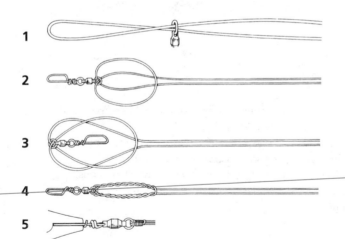

Offshore swivel knot: Used for attaching a swivel or snap to a doubled line, generally for trolling and saltwater fishing.
    1. Slip loop through swivel eye. Rotate loop end a half turn to put single
    twist in line.
    2. Fold loop over doubled line, with twist intact.
    3. Rotate swivel through center of loops at least six times.
    4. Release and slowly pull on swivel to gather loops into knot.
    5. Draw knot tight by pulling on ends and pushing loops into knot.
Courtesy of Stren.

There are several special knots that are used to connect one length of line to another. Frequently this involves joining lines of different diameters.

- **Blood knot:** Used by fly fishers to taper leaders from a heavy butt section to a light tippet using successively lighter sections of monofilament. The blood knot can be used to join any two monofilament lines provided they are not too dissimilar in diameter. It has high knot strength.

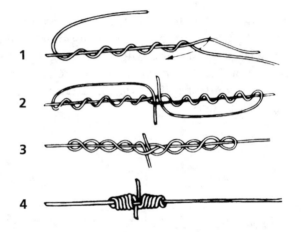

Blood knot
1. Overlap lines and wrap one end five times around standing line, tucking line end between the two lines.
2. Make second wrap of other line around remaining standing line, and tuck through same spot in opposite direction.
3. Moisten knot and begin to pull tight to shape coils.
4. Pull knot tight, snug and tighten ends, and trim.
Courtesy of Ande.

- **Double-strand blood knot:** Formed just like the blood knot, except that one strand is first doubled, then twisted around the other strand and knotted. It is best used when the two strands to be joined are of markedly different diameters. (Always double the smaller-diameter line.)
- **Surgeon's knot:** Also strong, and useful for joining lines of varying diameters. It is easy to tie—nothing more than an overhand knot with an added turn.

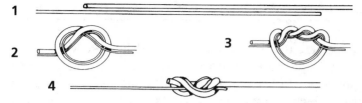

Surgeon's knot
1. Overlap two lines or line and leader.
2. Make overhand knot in the two overlapping lines.
3. Make second turn of both lines through overhand knot.
4. Hold both tag ends and pull knot tight. Trim.
Courtesy of Stren.

- **Surgeon's loop knot:** Strong and easy to tie, it involves only doubling the end of the line, then tying an overhand knot with an extra turn—just like the surgeon's knot.

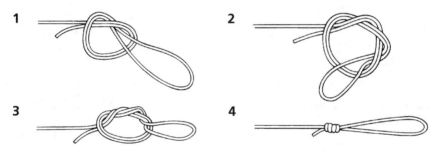

Surgeon's loop knot
1. Double end of line and, with it, make overhand knot.
2. Bring loop end through overhand knot a second time.
3. Pull on standing line and tag end (together) and loop end.
4. Moisten knot, pull tight, and trim tag end.
Courtesy of Berkley.

Doubling a line will create a strong and reliable leader. Here are some popular knots for this purpose.

- **Bimini twist:** One of the few that is as strong as the line—it is a 100 percent knot. Use the Bimini twist to double your line before you tie it to hook, lure, or leader—and when you want maximum strength out of all connections. It is often used to tie heavy tackle to a swivel (using the offshore swivel knot) or to a heavy leader (using the Albright). Tying the Bimini twist does requires practice, but it is not a difficult knot. The secret is to roll the line evenly over the twisted part of the two strands, and to use care when tying off the ends to secure the knot.

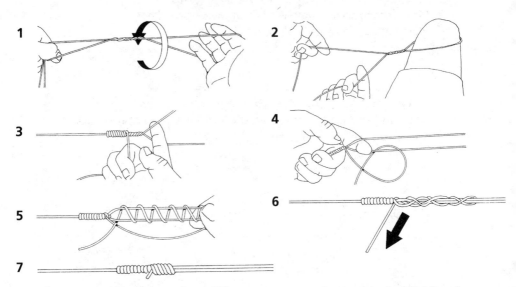

Bimini twist: Used to make a 100 percent strong knot with doubled line for tying to lures or leaders.

1. Fold over 3 or 4 feet of line end to make loop. Rotate loop 20 times to put twist in doubled line.
2. Spread loop and slip it over one knee. Pull ends to force the twisted line into tight twist.
3. Keep tension on loop with knee and roll tag end of line over the tight twists of line by pulling up on the loop with your index finger. Roll these turns until you reach end of the twisted line.
4. With line rolled to end of twist, make a half hitch to one side of loop (single line) to lock twisted line in place. Make a second half hitch around other strand of loop.
5. Secure knot by making a loop, then three or more turns (six are best) around *both* strands of loop, tucking tag end into the loops formed.
6. Remove loop from your knee, slip it over a narrow object (cleat, doorknob), and gently pull on tag end to secure final hitch. Pull gently back on them to make sure they slide up evenly.
7. The finished Bimini twist will look like this.

Courtesy of Stren.

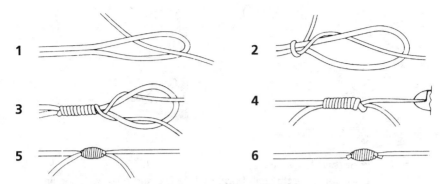

Albright knot: Used to join heavy line and wire to monofilament.
1. Form loop in heavy monofilament or wire, then insert monofilament through or parallel to this loop.
2. Pinch tight monofilament in finger and begin to wrap around the doubled heavy line/leader.
3. After 12 or more turns, tuck tag end through loop in heavy line/leader.
4. Slide coils of monofilament toward end of loop to lock tag end in loop.
5. Pull knot tight.
6. Trim ends. (An added touch is to make several loop hitches around standing line with tag end before trimming.)
Courtesy of Ande.

Wire knots are obviously more difficult to handle than those created from monofilament. They are used with heavier tackle and must withstand far greater line stress. Here is one example.

- **Figure-eight knot:** An easy knot with which to join braided wire to a hook or lure; it also allows you to undo the knot and retie it without clipping. Be sure to pull up on the *tag end,* not the standing wire. This knot will not work for single-strand wire.

There are thousands of other knots, but here are a few more that you may find useful.

- **In-line dropper loop:** Inserted anywhere in a line, this loop is useful for attaching a snelled hook or leader with interconnecting loops. An ideal way to make a quick jigging or bottom rig is to place one or more of these knots near the end of the line, then tie on an appropriate sinker (or add a jig on the loop to make a jigging rig). Making a very large loop and then cutting one leg can form a dropper, or provide a length of leader to snell a hook.

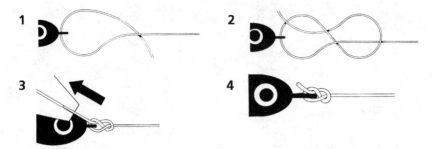

Figure-eight knot (braided wire *only*).
1. Insert braided wire through hook or lure eye and over standing line.
2. Wrap half turn around standing line then back through formed loop.
3. Pull *tag end* of line.
4. Cut excess wire with fishing pliers.
Courtesy of Stren.

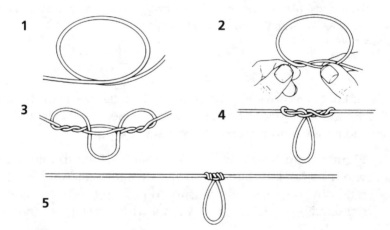

In-line dropper loop: This allows you to make a loop for snells or rigs anywhere in the middle of the line.
1. Overlap line to form loop.
2. Repeatedly turn overlapping strands five complete times.
3. Place loop through center opening of twisted strands.
4. Hold loop with your teeth and pull both ends of line.
5. Pull lines tightly to set knot and to make loop stand out perpendicular to line.
Courtesy of Ande.

- **Nail knot:** A knot with several variations, but all are used to attach a heavy leader to the end of a fly line. Wrap the monofilament around the end of the fly line, and hold a nail or a bit of tube along the line to support the wraps made around it while you tie the knot, then tuck the end through the loop parallel to the nail. Remove the nail and pull tight.

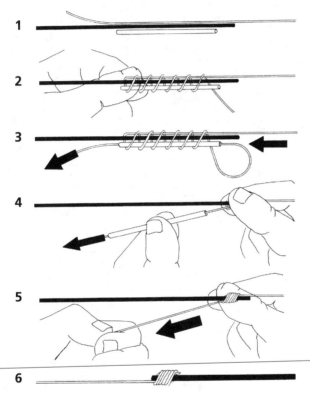

Tube nail knot
1. Lay tube (or small-diameter straw) alongside overlapping fly-line end and leader butt.
2. Hold all three pieces and make 10 wraps of leader butt around leader, tube, and fly line.
3. Tuck tag end of leader through tube.
4. Hold knot while sliding tube out of knot.
5. Alternately pull tag end and leader butt to snug knot.
6. Snug knot and clip ends; soak with sealer to protect.
Courtesy of Stren.

Several companies now manufacture special wire forms or sleeves and glue to make no-knot attachments. Wire or double-braid lines are often joined, or attachment loops made, by crimping on special leader sleeves using crimping pliers. As mentioned earlier, check with your dealer to make sure that your crimping pliers work with the sleeves you have chosen. Uncoated and nylon-coated wire, for example, require different sleeves even though both are of the same pound test.

Freshwater and Saltwater Baits

BEFORE YOU USE any bait, always check local regulations. Some areas prohibit the use of goldfish (carp), for example, because they can easily take over prime bass waters. To increase survival among released fish, many trout waters prohibit the use of baits (which the fish tend to swallow along with the hook), and restrict fishing to flies or lures. Check local restrictions about gathering baits as well; taking baits from trout streams is prohibited in many areas.

Many baits are used in both freshwater and saltwater fishing. Here are some examples.

Chunks of fish can be cut into strips, fillets, or bite-size pieces for bait.

Here a small chunk of baitfish is threaded onto a hook with the point of the hook showing.

Strips of bait are ideal when chumming or fishing the mid-depths. The thin, cigar-shaped strip will sink more readily than the wide fillet, thus allowing adjustment for current or tide.

- **Cut baits:** Chunks or slices of fish make good baits for still fishing, drift fishing, or bottom fishing. Small fish are often cut into pieces and hooked through the skin to help keep them in place. Larger fish are sometimes filleted first (leaving the skin on, but removing the scales), then cut into smaller chunks. Long, thin, tapered strips cut from a fillet or section of the belly work well for many species. Hook them through the skin at the thick end of the triangle.

- **Prepared baits:** Commercially available baits include paste-like concoctions that are specially formulated for carp, catfish, crappies, and other popular species. These baits are often scooped directly from the tin and molded onto a bait hook, which may be a single hook with barbs or a treble with a spring baitholder attachment. You can prepare simple home-made baits using cheese, dough, or blood-based formulas. Prepared baits are widely used in both fresh and salt water, primarily for bottom-feeding species.
- **Doughballs:** A type of prepared bait, easily made at home. They are a favorite of carp but also useful for other bottom-feeding fish, such as suckers or catfish. Doughballs are made of bread dough or a similar tough, doughy mix that can be easily molded onto a hook and will hold up when continually soaked.

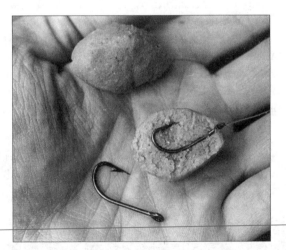

A doughball, cut open to show the hook. The dough hides the hook so that the fish will more readily take it.

Commercial dough is available for making doughballs, but here are two easy and effective formulas. The first is for strawberry-flavored carp dough, since carp seem to like strawberries. Dissolve 2 or 3 table-spoons of strawberry gelatin in 2 cups of boiling water (sugar can also be added to sweeten). Mix 2 cups of dry cornmeal and 1 cup of flour, add to the water-flavor solution, and mix well until it reaches a tough, doughy consistency.

Another favorite is Champion carp dough. Mix 1 cup each of Wheaties cereal, flour, oatmeal, and molasses. Add 1 cup of hot water and a small amount of vanilla extract. Mix thoroughly, once again aiming for a tough, moldable consistency. (One way to keep dough from breaking down is to carefully add bits of raw cotton balls to the mix to give it strength and body.)

Each fishing region seems to have its own slightly different version of the doughball. Some of the more exotic flavors include anise, beer, crushed canned corn, raspberry, licorice, cheese, and honey. They can all be stored in zipper-lock plastic bags or aluminum foil, and most of the fishing techniques are similar. Simply place the dough on the hook in grape-size balls, using a single hook or a treble hook with a spring (baitholder).

- **Shrimp:** Shrimp are an all-purpose bait for salt water and fresh water. Even if unavailable from inland baitshops, they can be purchased at most food markets. Small shrimp can be used whole, with live ones hooked through the forward part of the tail so the vital parts are not pierced. They can also be hooked through the middle of the tail. Dead shrimp, if small enough, can be threaded completely onto a hook, the point running out through the tail so the tail curves naturally. You can hook

Shrimp can be cut up into bait sections, using chunks or the tail, as shown here.

the tails of larger shrimp the same way, first removing the shell or slightly crushing the body to release its scent and increase its attractiveness in the water. Or you can cut the tails into smaller chunks and impale them on the hook.

Shrimp chunks and tails are often used to "sweeten" lures used in both fresh- and saltwater fishing. Here, shrimp is being added to a jig.

- **Grass shrimp:** These small shrimp are found inshore and in brackish water, and are available from bait dealers or by seining them from shallow shoreline areas. They are used live and whole; thread one or more through the body or tail onto a hook for perch, striped bass, and other inshore species.
- **Worms:** Earthworms, manure worms, and red worms are commonly used in freshwater and sometimes in saltwater fishing. Live worms are hooked whole or broken into smaller bits and threaded onto a hook; two or three small worms may also be threaded through the thicker collar on the body. You can use larger worms such as nightcrawlers with a two- or three-hook gang rig, threading one large worm onto all the hooks. Bass and catfish are often caught by using a mass of wriggling worms threaded onto one hook. Earthworms will not last as long in salt water as in fresh water, but they are a popular substitute for the more expensive bloodworms and sandworms available in coastal baitshops.

Small grass shrimp.

Simple worm riggings can include threading the hook through the length of the body, or through one or two spots, as shown here.

To completely hide a hook, thread several worms onto the shank and cover the point as much as possible.

- **Freshwater minnows:** Almost any type of freshwater minnow
  or small fish can be used as bait. Minnows, chubs, dace, shiners,
  and other species are sold in baitshops, and minnows can be net-
  ted from ponds or small streams. (In most cases you will need a
  fishing license, so check local restrictions.) Ways to gather minnows include minnow traps baited with crumbs and grain, dip
  nets baited the same way, or seines run by one or two anglers
  through the water and then lifted to capture the contents.

  The best way to hook minnows depends on how you are
  going to fish them. For casting and retrieving, trolling, or drifting
  minnows, hook them vertically through both lips. For drifting,
  also try hooking through the tail. When you are fishing a minnow under a bobber, hook through the back, just forward of the
  dorsal fin, but take care not to damage the spinal cord.

  Minnows can also be hooked onto some lures, such as jigs.
  One trick is to lip-hook a minnow upside down on a lightweight
  jig so the bait constantly struggles to regain an upright position.
  This struggle is sure to attract gamefish and provoke strikes.

Three ways to hook minnows (top to bottom): through the back for still fishing
with a bobber, through the tail to allow the minnow to swim and attract fish, and
through the lips when trolling or casting.

An upside down lip-hooked minnow on a jig will constantly try to right itself, making for more strikes.

Eels can be used fresh or salted and preserved, rigged whole through the lips or eyes or cut into chunks for still fishing and bottom fishing.

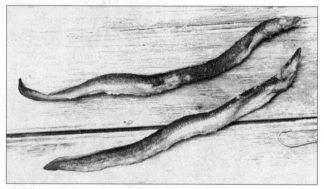

Live baitfish are often used to attract large saltwater gamefish. This bait has been hooked through the forward back, taking care not to damage the spinal cord.

- **Saltwater minnows:** Mullets, herring, menhaden, sardines (West Coast), candlefish (West Coast), spearing (Northeast Coast), killifish, anchovies, alewives, pinfish, smelt, silversides, sand eels, and similar baitfish are popular in coastal waters. Most are available from live-bait dealers or can be caught using a dip net, short seine, or cast net.

   Typical hooking methods are similar to those for freshwater minnows: through the lips in a vertical plane (trolling, deep jigging, or casting), through the back (drifting and still fishing, but be careful to avoid the spine to keep the bait lively), and through the wrist of the tail for drifting and fishing tides.

   Another method is hooking the bait through the side. For this technique, run a long-shank hook through the mouth, out the gill, and into the side of the fish near the tail. Or run a double hook, eye-first, up through the vent and out the mouth, where you tie or connect it to a line or leader. For trolling, use a large hook and attach the minnow side to side through the eyes or securely through the top and bottom lips. Use dead minnows with these methods.

In both freshwater (catfish) and much saltwater fishing, a good way to hook dead minnows is to run a double hook through the vent and out the mouth, then attach a leader or tie on the line.

- **Adult insects:** These are good baits if they are easy to catch, are large enough to be impaled onto a hook, and are local food that fish would normally eat. Good examples include crickets, grasshoppers, beetles, leafhoppers, dragonflies, damselflies, dobsonflies, and crane flies. Crickets, grasshoppers, and beetles are relatively easy to catch; dragonflies and damselflies may require nets and some ingenuity. Hook insects through the abdomen to hide the hook, or through the back of the thorax with an exposed hook. This keeps the insect living longer and acting naturally. Occasionally a very light split-shot sinker is helpful when you fish with insects.

Crickets and other insects can be threaded individually (top) or in multiples (bottom) onto a light-wire hook, as shown, for catching trout and panfish.

- **Immature insects:** Aquatic, immature (nymphal) forms of insects are also useful as baits. Large nymphs of mayflies, stoneflies, and caddis (the insects that form cases of wood or stone) make ideal baits. Hellgrammites (larvae of the dobsonfly) are preferred by smallmouth bass and large trout. Hook these insects through the back of the thorax. Immature terrestrial insects (beetles, crickets) can also be effective baits.
- **Frogs:** Frogs and toads are now thought to be threatened by ultraviolet light from a thinning ozone layer, as well as by acid precipitation. We therefore do not recommend wild specimens

as baits. However, if a bait dealer can *verify that they were raised, not captured in the field,* then frogs are suitable bait for bass and pike. Hook them through the lip if casting or trolling; through the leg if drifting or still fishing.

Mealworms, available from bait-shops, can be threaded individually and lengthwise onto a hook; or thread them through the body, as shown, for multiple hooking and a large bait.

- **Salamanders:** These and other amphibians also suffer a threatened existence, so only commercially raised baits should be used. Hook them through the lips. Small sizes are often used for trout, while larger specimens such as mud puppies or hellbenders are used for bass and walleyes.

A salamander may be hooked through the lips or a front leg.

- **Leeches:** These are ideal baits, especially for walleyes and smallmouth bass. Where they are abundant, they can be caught in streams and ponds; or buy them from a bait dealer. Hook them through the front (head), or by threading the hook through the body. Leeches are effective on lures or on a single hook while drifting or using a bait-walking rig.

Leeches are best hooked through the forward part so that they swim naturally in the water.

- **Crawfish:** These are great baits for almost all freshwater fish, including trout, smallmouth and largemouth bass, panfish, walleyes, and catfish. Crawfish can be used whole or in parts. Hook whole crawfish through the back of the thorax or by threading the hook through the tail, with the bend of the hook following the natural bend of the tail. To use parts (for small-mouthed fish, or from large crawfish), cut the tail into short pieces and use as you would shrimp, threading a small chunk onto a hook. The entire tail can also be used; thread it onto a suitable hook. A light in-line sinker is sometimes helpful to get the crawfish down to where the fish are feeding.
- **Marshmallows:** A simple and effective bait for trout, panfish, carp, and catfish. Most anglers use the "mini" or marble-size marshmallows, but the large standard size can also be cut into chunks. Thread one onto a hook, burying all of the shank and point. Or slice halfway through a marshmallow, slip it over the line and hook shank, then slide it down to bury all three points of a treble hook.
- **Cheese:** Cut into chunks, this is an ideal bait for many species, including panfish, catfish, carp, and even trout. Kraft's Velveeta brand is preferred by many anglers, since it has a smooth consistency, cuts easily, and threads well onto hooks. However, some cheeses with a similar consistency work equally well.

One or more chunks of bait can be placed on a hook, depending on the size of the hook.

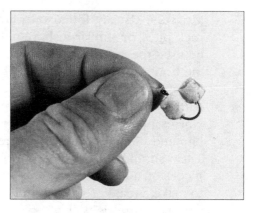

• **Clams:** A wide variety of clams is found along saltwater and freshwater shores. They are most effective when you are bottom fishing with a single- or double-hook bottom rig. Whole clams can be used, or small parts can be cut up and threaded onto a hook (make sure that as much of the shank and point are covered as possible). Clams are often difficult to hold on a hook; it helps to remove the bait from the shell to let it harden and toughen in the sun and air for a few minutes. However, do not allow it to dry out completely or become brittle.

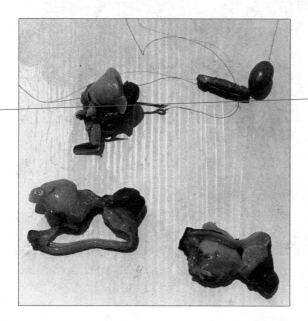

Clams are ideal for saltwater fishing and freshwater bottom fishing (using freshwater mussels), and are best hooked by threading the hook several times through the body of the clam.

- **Mussels:** Usually found on pilings, bridge abutments, jetties, rock piles, or similar inshore and tidal structures, mussels can be used the same way as clams. Thread the entire mussel onto the hook or cut it up into smaller pieces to thread onto small hooks.
- **Bloodworms and other sea worms:** Bloodworms, sandworms, pile worms, clam worms, cinder worms, and others can bite and pinch, so beware of the front end of these creatures. They should be handled carefully and placed whole or in pieces on a hook. Several can be threaded onto one large hook to make a mass of worms, which will attract larger fish. Or use a single-worm rig with a series of three hooks on a leader, each hook an inch or so apart, and impale the worm by its tail, head, and middle onto the three hooks.
- **Sand fleas:** Sometimes called sand crabs or mole crabs, these small, shell-backed, crablike creatures are usually found right at the surf line. Sand fleas are easily captured by digging along

Bloodworms are a saltwater bait used for bottom fishing and still fishing in salt water; cut them into pieces, as shown here, or thread them completely onto a hook.

this wash line, and are good baits for surf fishing. They can be threaded singly or in multiples onto a hook.

- **Strip baits:** These are nothing more than strips of fish, often from those caught but not wanted, or from the belly of fish that have been filleted or cleaned. The best strips are from small fish. Fillet out each side and trim into a long triangle. Remove the scales to make it easy to hook once through the skin, or back and forth several times on long strips with long-shank hooks. Such strips can be made in any size to suit the fishing—as small as ¼ inch wide and 1 inch long, and up to an inch or more wide and 4 to 6 inches long. Ideal for trolling, and bottom rigs or dropper rigs.

Strips from the belly of a caught fish (top) or a chunk with the tail intact (bottom).

- **Squid:** A popular saltwater bait, squid can be used whole by running the line through the mantle (use a bait-threading needle) and hooking in the head. Larger squid can be cut into crosswise circles; these can then be made into tapered pieces as strip baits. A squid's head can also be used on a larger rig by hooking it through the eyes. Squid are popular for trolling, as well as any bottom rig, float rig, or basic rig.

Squid are best fished by cutting into chunks for threading onto a hook or making strips for trolling.

- **Octopi:** Like squid, octopi can be used whole in small sizes, or you can cut the tentacles into sections to use as chunk bait or into long sections for use as strip baits. Octopi are tough and an ideal saltwater bait.
- **Conches and whelks:** These large shellfish are good eating for humans but can also be used as bait. Cut the tough bodies into chunks for small fish, or use the bait whole and thread it onto a hook for larger fish.
- **Eels:** Ideal baits for a number of inshore and coastal species, they can be used whole and live for trolling for striped bass and other coastal species: Simply hook them through the eyes or lips. Chunks of eel are also a tough and useful bait for bottom fishing. Cut the eel into suitable-size pieces and thread them through the skin onto a hook. (Eels also make ideal crab baits in traps, in pots, or on trotlines.)
- **Crabs:** Hard-shell, soft-shell, and peeler crabs are all good saltwater baits. Hard-shell crabs are best fished by cutting them into pieces. First twist the legs off at the body; each leg can then be further broken or cut into small sections for bait. Next, pull up the apron and peel off the back at the same time. Cut the crab in half, then cut each half into smaller sections. Soft-shell and peeler crabs are better for baits, since they

are easier for most fish species to eat. They are cut and
hooked the same way as hard-shell crabs. Crabs, like a number
of other fragile baits, are not suitable for trolling. Similarly, use
care when casting, since these baits do not stay on the hook
well. Use a gentle, loblike cast, or try rigging the bait with a
rubber band or string.

Crabs can be torn apart and cut into chunks for still fishing.

CHAPTER

Bait Rigs

A LMOST ANY BAIT RIG can theoretically be used for any kind of fishing, but some are obviously intended for fresh water and some for salt water. As a result, there many variations in hooks, leader lengths and styles, sizes and positions of sinkers, and so on. However, our focus here is on basic rigs. The main concerns in choosing any rig are whether you will be casting and retrieving, drifting a bait, fishing with a float, bottom fishing with a sinker, or trolling.

CLICKING
NOISE →

SPLIT-SHOT →

NEEDLE-NOSE
WORM WEIGHTS

18 INCHES

HOOK

BAIT

Sometimes several sinkers are better than one, such as when you are using several small sinkers, or using a sinker with a series of beads that will clatter or click to make noise as you hop and bounce a bait along the bottom.
Cliff Shelby.

All bait rigs incorporate a line or leader, a hook or hooks, and often a sinker and/or float (bobber). Some rigs also require a separate line or leader (dropper) to hold a hook coming off the main line. All rig components, however, need to be joined using one of the common methods described below.

Use a three-way swivel by tying the line to one of its eyes, the leader with the hook (or snelled hook) to its second eye, and a snap with a sinker to its third eye. A variation of this method is to tie a short leader to the third eye that is tied to another three-way swivel. This creates a second hook rig. Three- and even four-hook rigs can be made this way. A standard swivel (with two eyes) can be used to tie the line and the hook snell (leader) to one eye, and the sinker or a second line to the other.

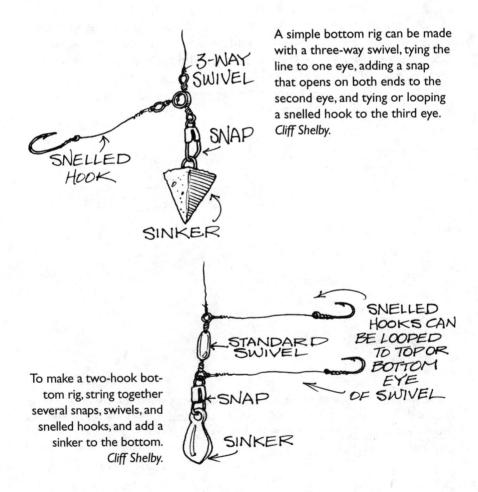

A simple bottom rig can be made with a three-way swivel, tying the line to one eye, adding a snap that opens on both ends to the second eye, and tying or looping a snelled hook to the third eye. *Cliff Shelby.*

To make a two-hook bottom rig, string together several snaps, swivels, and snelled hooks, and add a sinker to the bottom. *Cliff Shelby.*

The knots discussed in chapter 2 are essential in making any type of rig. For example, you can tie an in-line dropper loop in the line wherever you want, pull it tight, and clip one end of the loop close to the knot. This becomes a separate leader for a hook attachment. Or tie an in-line dropper loop but, instead of clipping the line, loop the end through the hook eye and around the hook to attach it. (To keep the hook straight with the line, you must use one with a turned-up or turned-down eye.)

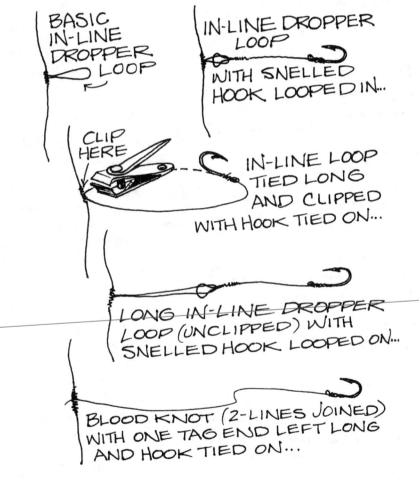

In-line dropper loops.
Cliff Shelby.

Here are two other possibilities. Tie an in-line dropper loop as above, but use it to interlock with the loop of a snelled hook instead of threading through the eye of a hook. Or tie a blood knot, leave one of its tag ends very long, and attach a hook to it.

Hook lears or spreaders are wire forms that you can buy or make; they extend the hook leader or snell out from the main line. A simple one can be made from light spring wire in the shape of an L on its side, with an eye formed at each end and at the bend in the L. Attach the line to the eye at one end of the L, the sinker or continuing line to the eye at the bend, and the hook leader or snell to the eye at the end of the second arm.

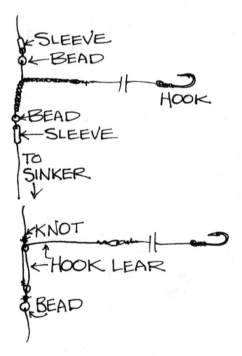

Commercial hook lears, available at tackle shops, allow you to make up your own rigs by adding lears to the line to form single- or multiple-hook rigs. Hook lears are extensions that help keep the snelled hooks away from the line and prevent tangling.
Cliff Shelby.

Float rigs use a float to suspend the baited hook at the desired depth above the bottom. The float, a sinker to submerge the bait, and the hook can all be in a straight line, or dropper leaders off the main line between the float and sinker can hold the hook and bait. This second method, preferred by many, also lets you use several droppers to fish at different depths or to try different baits.

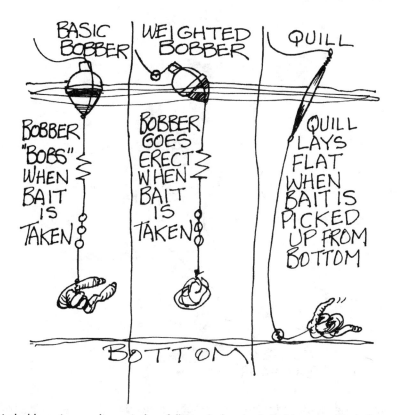

Basic bobber rigs can be varied as follows: Left, a basic bobber that "bobs" up and down as the bait is taken; center, a weighted bobber that springs up from lying on its side when the bait is taken or moved; and right, a quill float that is rigged to sit vertically with a suspended bait and will lie on its side when the bait is picked up by a fish. *Cliff Shelby.*

Float rigs can be awkward or dangerous to cast if you are fishing with line going more than about 3 feet deep. In these instances, a bobber stop will allow you to use a float while fishing very deep. Add a small stop to the line; you can reel this in with your line on most tackle. The stop can be as simple as a rubber band tied onto the line, or a small spring or rubber bead (available through tackle dealers) that is threaded onto it. The line is also threaded through a small sliding bead big enough to block the sliding float. The bead and float slide to the end of the line before your cast. When you do cast this outfit, the weight of the sinker and the baited hook pull the line through the float and bead until both are halted by the small bobber stop.

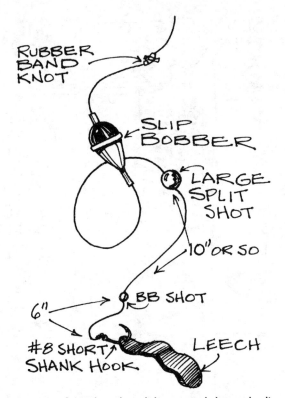

RUBBER
BAND
KNOT

SLIP
BOBBER

LARGE
SPLIT
SHOT

10" OR SO

BB SHOT

6"

#8 SHORT
SHANK HOOK

LEECH

Slip bobber rigs consist of a sinker that slides up and down the line, ending with a sinker and bait rig, as shown. A rubber band knotted or tied to the line, or a commercial bobber stop rig, will prevent the bobber from sliding all the way up the line yet still make casting possible when you are fishing deep.
Cliff Shelby.

Systems such as this allow you to use a wide variety of floats, from simple round plastic devices to the longer and more sensitive European-type floats. The best bobber systems use just enough weight to sink the bait and allow casting, and a bobber with just enough buoyancy to keep it floating. Both allow for maximum sensitivity to the feel when a fish takes the hook. Such rigs are used mostly for fishing with baits. However, they are also excellent for fishing with such lures as jigs or bait-tipped jigs at a certain depth, particularly for crappies or perch.

Bottom-fishing rigs (similar to float rigs but without the float) can be fished right on the bottom or suspended vertically from a boat, bridge, pier, jetty, or other structure to fish the mid-depths. In its simplest form, a bottom-fishing rig consists of an in-line sinker, such as a rubber core or pinch-on, with the end of the line tied to a hook. The bait rests on the bottom, unless you add a float to the end of the line (next to the hook) to suspend the bait.

A simple one-hook bottom rig can be made by tying a hook to the end of the line, then adding a pinch-on or rubber-core sinker anywhere along the line.
Cliff Shelby.

Many bottom rigs use droppers off the main line to hold the hook, with a sinker tied to the end of the main line. Such rigs can be bought or made using three-way swivels, standard swivels, or knots.

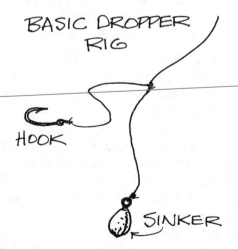

Cutting the line allows you to tie a blood knot with a long tag end for tying on a hook, while tying the sinker to the end of the line.
Cliff Shelby.

A two-hook bottom rig adds a second dropper or leader above the first. Three hooks are sometimes fished this way, but rarely more. To avoid tangling the hooks, keep the upper dropper line shorter than the distance between the line connection and the lower hook connection.

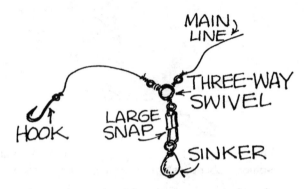

Simple bottom rigs can be made with a three-way swivel, as shown. *Cliff Shelby.*

Which sinker to use in a bottom rig depends on the type of bottom, as well as the weight required to hold the rig and counteract the tide or current (see chapter 1 for sinker suggestions). Similarly, hooks vary in size and type with the species sought (also see chapter 1).

Here are five simple possibilities for bottom rigs.

- Tie a hook to the end of the line, and add a pinch-on or rubber-core sinker 12 to 24 inches above it. The sinker will keep the hook on the bottom. When fished above the bottom, the bait will drift with the current or tide.
- Tie a sinker to the end of the line, then tie in an in-line dropper loop. Add the hook by running the loop through the hook eye, interlocking it with a loop-eye snelled hook, or cutting one end of the loop and tying it to the hook.
- Make a two-hook bottom rig as above, but with two dropper loops in the line.
- Buy single- or two-hook bottom rigs for your fishing. These consist of a swivel or eye to which you tie the line, a snap on the bottom to hold a sinker, and two arms or hook lears to hold hooks or snells.

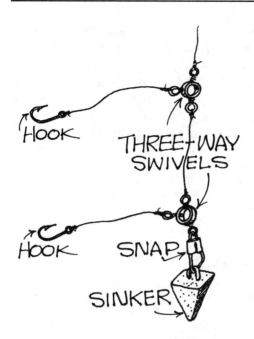

HOOK

THREE-WAY SWIVELS

HOOK SNAP

SINKER

Using two three-way swivels and a double-ended snap enables you to make up simple two-hook bottom rigs with any desired spacing between the hooks. They can be tied with regular monofilament line, or heavier monofilament for increased strength and durability.
Cliff Shelby.

- Spreader rigs are used primarily for shallow saltwater flounder fishing, as well as freshwater perch and panfish. These usually consist of a center line-tie, a snap for a sinker directly under the line-tie, and two to four arms on which leaders or snelled hooks can be added. They are usually fished to hold baits where the fish are located—either on the bottom for flounder, or at mid-depths for perch, panfish, and crappies.

Spreader rigs, available from coastal tackle shops, are widely used to fish several baits for bottom species such as fluke, flounder, and sea bass. Snelled hooks are added to the end of the wire frame arms.
Cliff Shelby.

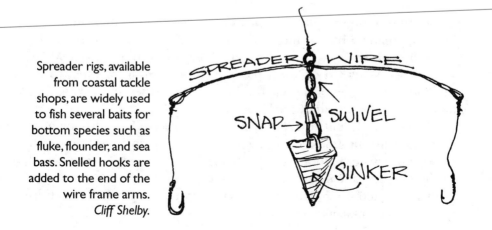

SPREADER WIRE

SNAP SWIVEL

SINKER

Drift-fishing rigs are similar to bottom rigs but have no weight—or less weight—to allow a bait to drag along behind a drifting boat. This allows you to cover more water when fishing and also helps you locate schools or pockets of fish. Drift-fishing rigs may also be used from an anchored boat in a current or tidal flow; the technique is to drift a bait by slowly releasing line from the reel. A light sinker will help get the bait down, and the multiple hooks help present the bait over a larger area.

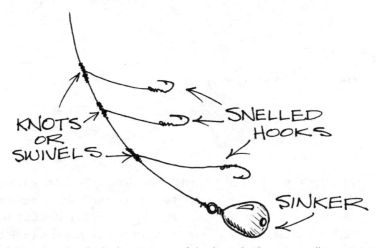

Drift-fishing rigs, in which the rig is not fished on the bottom, still require sinkers to keep the baits down. Here the snelled hooks can be attached using swivels or in-line dropper loops.
Cliff Shelby.

Another type of drift rig uses a sinker designed to drag along the bottom, pulling a bait or lure as the boat drifts. The weight is usually tapered or fixed to a long wire that slides along the bottom. Many anglers use V-shaped or safety-pin-type wires that allow them to tie the line to the apex of the V, and then tie the leader and lure or bait to the unweighted end of the V.

Trolling with bait usually involves strip baits, whole fish, or minnows that are lip-hooked or sewn onto a hook so they track well through the water without twisting line. Some trolling rigs are designed so the bait actually skips on the surface (as in big-game fishing), but most are fished deep. Trolling rigs are also used with lures such as spoons, jigs, crankbaits, and soft plastics.

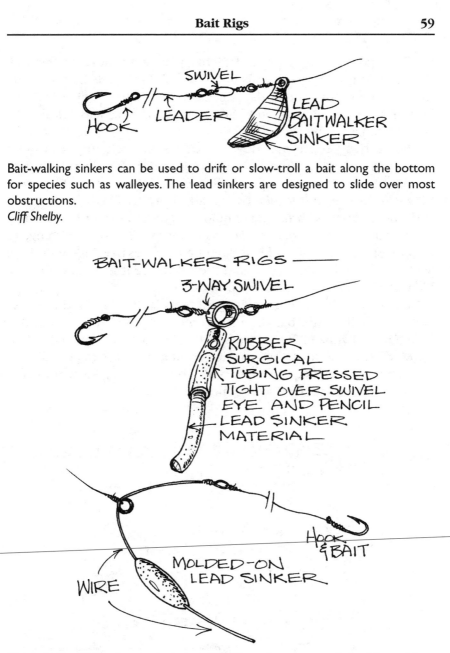

Bait-walking sinkers can be used to drift or slow-troll a bait along the bottom for species such as walleyes. The lead sinkers are designed to slide over most obstructions.
Cliff Shelby.

Other bait-walking rigs can include a T style or three-way swivel with a rubber-hose sleeve attached to one eye to hold pencil lead. The length and diameter of the lead can be varied to adjust for the desired weight. Bottom-fishing sinkers molded onto a wire (sometimes straight, sometimes like a safety pin, as shown) allow you to fish the bottom with minimal chance of hanging up.
Cliff Shelby

Planers—sometimes called diving planes, because of the way they dive in the water—are also used to fish both baits and lures. Tie the line to the front end of the plane, and the leader (ending with the lure or bait) to the back end. Various triggering devices release the plane when a fish hits.

Some rigs keep a bait down with a sinker. This is positioned either in-line between the line and long leader, or suspended a few inches to a few feet off the third eye of a three-way swivel tied between the line and leader. The length of leader between the hook and sinker varies with fishing conditions. For freshwater fishing, only a few feet of leader is needed. For some types of saltwater fishing, up to 30 feet or more of leader is sometimes necessary. Rigs with long leaders require handlining to land the fish, since it is usually impossible to reel in past the sinker fixed to the rig.

Some baitfish-trolling rigs require special rigging of the bait. A good example is the ballyhoo rig commonly used for trolling this long-beaked baitfish. A wire leader is attached to the hook with a haywire twist, the end of the haywire ending with a straight "pin" or right-angle projection. A separate wire—often copper—is wrapped to the hook eye and used to secure the bait.

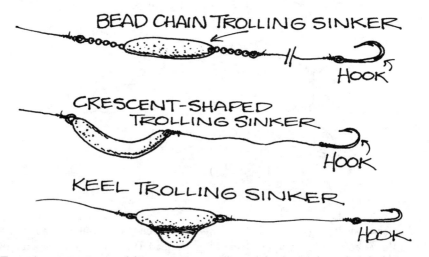

To reduce rotation and line twisting, trolling sinkers can have bead chains, as with the cigar sinker (top); or they can be specially shaped, as with the crescent sinker (middle) and keel-trolling sinker (bottom).
Cliff Shelby.

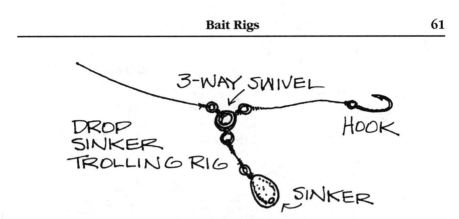

One way to keep a lure or bait at a given depth right off the bottom is to use a drop sinker rig, in which a sinker is tied to a line that in turn is tied to a three-way swivel. Line length for the sinker can range from a few inches to 5 or more feet. *Cliff Shelby.*

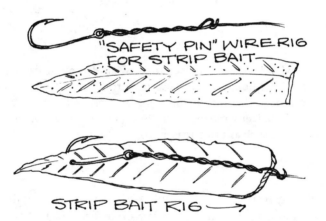

To troll strip baits, use a wire leader in which the wire is twisted together to hold a hook, then the end is used to attach the upper end of the strip bait. The hook is placed through the tail of the bait.
Cliff Shelby.

The ballyhoo is actually hooked through the gills, then down into the belly, and out the belly or vent. On other species, hook through the mouth and out the belly. The leader's right-angle pin impales the head of the bait; you then use the copper wire to wrap the nose or beak of the baitfish to the wire leader. After you have secured the head, finish the rig by wrapping the wire around the forward part of the wire leader.

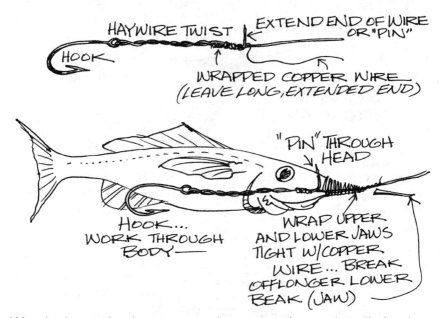

HAYWIRE TWIST ← EXTEND END OF WIRE OR "PIN"

HOOK

WRAPPED COPPER WIRE (LEAVE LONG, EXTENDED END)

"PIN" THROUGH HEAD

HOOK... WORK THROUGH BODY—

WRAP UPPER AND LOWER JAWS TIGHT W/COPPER WIRE... BREAK OFF LONGER LOWER BEAK (JAW)

Wire leaders with a haywire twist (wire twisted around itself after being threaded through the hook eye) are also used to hold trolling baitfish, with the hook worked through the body or out through a gill and hooked into the side, then the head of the bait wrapped with the tag end of the wire. This is ideal for slim-headed baitfish such as balao (ballyhoo).
Cliff Shelby.

Another way to rig a free-swimming bait is to use heavy thread and a needle. Secure the thread to the hook with a series of half hitches, then run the needle and thread alternately through the lips and eyes of the baitfish, securing it with half hitches to the hook. Your sewing thread thus forms a sling through the front of the bait, with its ends attached to the bend of the hook on each side of the baitfish's head. Eels are often hooked this way, or by hooking straight through the eyes or lips.

Surf fishermen can use single- or two-hook bottom rigs as described above, or a different and useful rig called the "fish-finder." This rig uses a sliding sinker connector, which allows a fish to take the bait without detecting the weight. To make this rig, run the line through the sliding sinker connector, then tie the line to a standard swivel. Tie a 24- to 30-inch leader with hook to the second eye of the swivel. The swivel will stop the sliding sinker (usually a pyramid or bank sinker), allowing smooth casting.

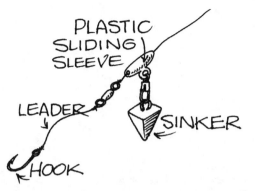

To allow fish to take a bait without dragging the sinker and perhaps dropping the bait, use a fish-finder rig. This employs a special sinker sleeve through which the line slides, as shown. These are widely available in coastal surf shops. For freshwater fishing, you can use the same rig with a snap swivel; the line goes through the eye of the swivel and the sinker attaches to the snap. Most rigs also use a swivel in the line to prevent the sinker from sliding down and tangling with the bait.
Cliff Shelby.

A similar rig for freshwater fishing (most often for catfish and carp) uses the same arrangement. Run the line through an egg sinker, tie the line to a swivel, and end with a 3-foot leader and a single hook.

Here a simple freshwater sliding-sinker rig uses an egg sinker. The line runs through the egg sinker then is tied to a swivel; next comes a length of leader, before you tie on the hook and add bait.
Cliff Shelby

Lure Rigs

L URES CAN BE CAST or trolled at the end of your fishing line, and often no other rigging is required. Whether you are fishing for freshwater or saltwater species, simply use your favorite line-to-lure knot. However, it is essential to work or retrieve all lures so that they resemble live, injured bait, or have an erratic action that singles them out from other baitfish. Such erratic action alerts game-fish to the lure, making strikes more likely. Try a mix of twitches, jerks, pauses, swimming motions, jigging actions, and similar movements.

Some lures are sold in bulk without any hook or other tackle and must be rigged before use. This is true of most soft-plastic lures. The Texas rig is basic to fishing any worm, lizard, crayfish, or other soft plastic for largemouth bass, smallmouth bass, walleyes, panfish, perch, trout, or catfish. The technique consists of tying the worm hook to the end of the line, threading the hook point straight into the head of the lure, bringing it out the side, then repositioning the hook point in the body of the worm.

The secret of an effective rigging is to make sure that the worm or lizard is straight on the hook, with no bends, kinks, or stretching. This is an ideal basic rig, but especially so for fishing in weeds or around snags and underwater structure. (A tapered worm weight can also be used to provide casting weight or to help sink the worm to where the fish are feeding.)

The Florida rig is much like the Texas rig, but the hook is threaded farther into the head of the worm so that it is kinked. The result is a worm that twists and swims in the water, although it can also twist the line unless you attach a swivel. A variation uses a

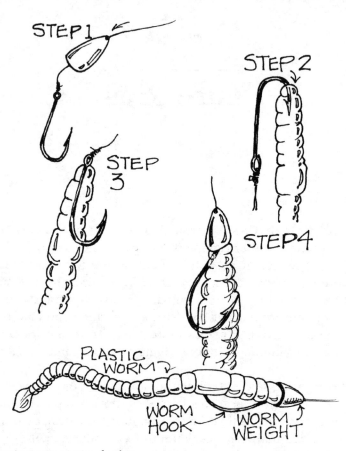

Basic plastic-worm rigging for bass:
1. Run line through tapered worm sinker and tie on hook.
2. Run point of hook straight into head of worm.
3. Bring point of hook out of worm's side so that only end of hook shank remains in the worm.
4. Insert point of hook back into worm's body to make it weedless.
Cliff Shelby.

barbed-shank, baitholder hook, with the point exposed and the worm extending partway down the hook bend to create the kink and the swimming motion. A ball-bearing swivel can be used to reduce line twist. This rig is best for open water, where the twisting, swimming motion will draw fish out and provoke strikes.

The rear-hook Texas rig is a variation, with the hook placed in the tail of the worm. One way is to tie the hook to the line, run the hook through and out the head of the worm, then into the body, repeating this several times as necessary, before turning it and sinking the point into the tail end of the worm.

An alternative is to run a very long needle (available from clothing and upholstery stores) eye-first up from the worm's tail and out the head, thread the line through the needle eye, and pull it back through the worm before tying on the hook. This is the best rig when fish are striking short—not taking the whole worm, or striking and running without getting a head-hooked worm in their mouth.

The Carolina rig uses either an exposed hook or a weedless hook rig (Texas rig) with a sliding bullet sinker on the line; you then tie the line to a swivel, and tie the swivel to a leader (often 24 to 30 inches long) that ends with the worm. It is difficult to cast and must be lobbed, but it is good for fishing deep in large lakes. It will take fish from deeper waters than any crankbait.

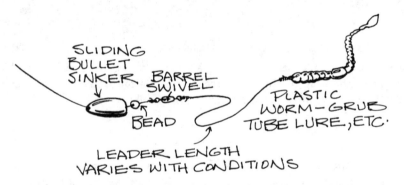

A basic Carolina rig can use a Texas-rigged (weedless) worm, or one with an exposed hook point. It is ideal for fishing deep, open water.
Cliff Shelby.

The wacky worm rig is fished most often around structure or in open water for suspended bass. When it moves through the water, it looks a lot like a live, writhing worm. Achieve this action by burying a lead worm weight or a small nail body in the head of the worm, then hooking the worm through the center with the point exposed. The weight causes the head of the worm to sink; when jigged, it will have a wacky up-and-down movement. This is an ideal rig for spotted bass or any fish that hold in deep, open water, along water edges, or near break lines.

Wacky worm rigs are made by hooking a plastic worm in the middle and adding a weight to the head to give it an erratic action in the water. Lead inserts are available commercially, or you can use a length of nail (shown here).

Any of the above rigs can be fished alone, or rigged with a tapered worm weight to get the lure down to the fish and to help penetrate weeds. Plastic worms sometimes require special tricks to rig correctly. Here are two tips that make worms easier to fish, regardless of the rig you use. First, peg the worm to the line by running a toothpick into the hole in the weight after threading it onto the line and tying and rigging the worm hook. Break off the toothpick to prevent snags. The peg will hold the weight in place and allow it to pound through weeds and sink the worm rapidly. The second tip is similar: To keep fish from taking a worm or soft-plastic lure and sliding it down the hook, hold the worm in place with a toothpick threaded through the head of the worm and the eye of the hidden hook.

Some lures require added weight or rigging to be cast properly or trolled at the correct depths. There are a number of solutions, including an in-line sinker positioned between the rod and the lure to help

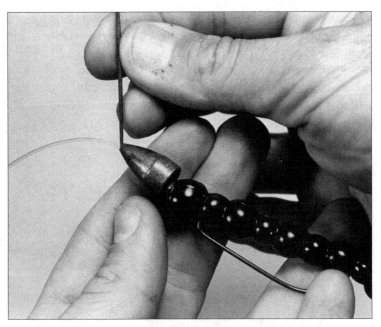

To hold a worm weight in place ahead of the worm, peg it with a toothpick. Pegs are also available commercially.

To prevent a worm from sliding down on a hook, peg the worm to the eye of the hook (as shown) after you thread the worm onto the hook. Break off ends of the toothpick before fishing.

get lures deep. If you are trolling, sinkers can be 30 feet or more ahead of the lure in salt water, but usually only a few feet in fresh water. With rigs designed for casting, such as the Carolina, the sinker should be carefully positioned: no closer than about 1 foot in front of the lure to prevent slowing the lure action, and no more than about 2 ½ feet ahead of it to allow for casting. Cast slowly and carefully, and make sure that you have complete clearance for the lure rig.

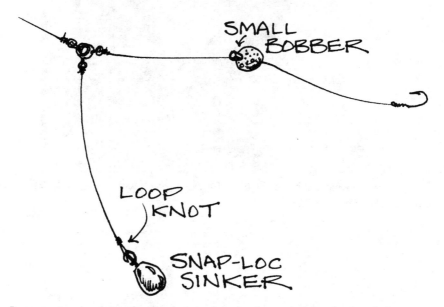

Bottom rigs that have the line, bait or lure leader, and sinker leader tied to sepa-rate eyes of a three-way swivel are effective and easy to make. The length of the leader from the swivel to the sinker controls the depth of the rig. Some bait rigs, especially when very slowly trolled, use a small bobber (as shown) to keep the bait visible to the fish and off the bottom.
Cliff Shelby.

Drop sinkers are used only in trolling, not casting, to keep the lure close to the bottom. Rig them by using a three-way swivel with the line tied to one eye, the lure tied by a leader to the second eye, and the sinker tied to a 1- to 3-foot leader to allow it to bounce along the bottom. (Note that fish caught on trolled lures with long leaders must be handlined to the boat, since the swivel cannot be reeled through the guides or onto the spool.)

Bait-walker rigs are similar to the drop-sinker rig, with a short leader and a special sinker that drags along the bottom during slow trolling or drifting. Bait-walker rigs are most often used in fresh water, with the lure close to the bottom.

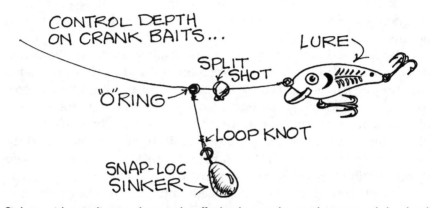

Sinkers, either in-line or drop-style off a leader, can be used to control the depth of a running lure that might otherwise float, never reaching the desired depths. A swivel or split shot, as shown, is used to keep the sinker away from the line-tie to the lure, and to make sure that the lure action is not compromised by the weight.
Cliff Shelby.

One way to make bottom rigs in snaggy water is to use a series of split shot on a separate leader off a swivel or tied from a dropper loop. Then, if the sinkers get caught, they will pull off so that the bait/hook or lure is not lost. Use a lighter-test sinker leader than you do in the main line.
Cliff Shelby

Deep-water trolling the mid-depths—for fish such as salmon and trout—is easy when you use a heavy sinker that stays deep when slow-trolled, combined with one or more lures fished off droppers that are several feet long. Attach them to the main line above the sinker using three-way swivels, blood knots, or dropper loops. This type of rig is often used to fish the thermocline—the layer of water separating the warmer upper waters and the colder, oxygen-poor depths.

Planers, used only for trolling, work similarly to the diving planes on submarines. When rigged between the rod and the lure, the planer and lures or bait are forced by the pressure of moving water deeper than they would ordinarily track. Most planers are equipped with a mechanical or magnetic catch that trips when a fish strikes. The planer then loses its diving capability until the fish is landed and the planer reset. Divers are similar to planers but feature an erratic side-to-side motion that gives the lure more action in the water.

Side planers are little floating "sleds" attached by a heavy line to a fixed point on the boat. Clips that release on a strike allow the planer to hold fishing line and trolling lures. Side planers are used primarily in large freshwater lakes for trolling multiple lines, or to get lures close to a shallow, rocky shoreline.

It is often effective to fish two lures in tandem on one line. Rig the added lure from a dropper, or from a leader running from the main lure to a trailing lure. The two lures are generally separated by a foot or two. Here are some possible combinations.

- A small jig behind a topwater (cupped-face) chugger or a floating-diver plug.
- Two jigs, one on the main line and one on a dropper.
- A small jig on a dropper in front of a diving crankbait—as if the crankbait were chasing the smaller jig.
- A small spoon on a dropper in front of a larger spoon.
- A large streamer fly followed by a nymph.
- A small nymph on a dropper in front of a streamer fly.
- A Texas-rigged plastic worm or grub on a dropper ahead of a jig.
- A small and large lure, or two same-size lures in different colors.

Lures are often "sweetened" with bait to increase strikes and catches. The bait should enhance the lure and not interfere with any built-in lure action. Some typical lure-and-bait combinations are:

- Spinners are often tipped with a piece of worm, bloodworm, small minnow, or strip bait cut from caught fish.
- Weedless spoons need thin baits such as strip baits, pork rinds, minnows, or leeches to avoid interfering with the spoon's side-to-side action.
- Trolling spoons are often tipped with strip baits or minnows.
- Soft plastics, such as the grubs often fished on jigs in salt water, can be tipped with a shrimp, shrimp tail, or bloodworm.
- Spinnerbaits and buzzbaits are commonly tipped with pork rinds or strip baits.

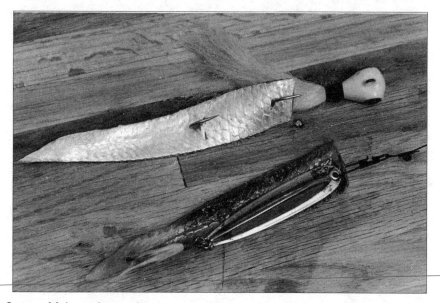

Strips of fish can be used to "sweeten" lures, such as the strip baits used on this jig and metal casting spoon.

- Heavy-structure spoons dropped to deep structure are often sweetened in salt water with shrimp, clams, clam snouts, strip baits, shiners, or bloodworms; in fresh water, with earthworms, small minnows, or leeches.
- In salt water, jigs are tipped with shrimp, bloodworms, minnows, strip baits, or clam snouts. In fresh water, they are tipped with earthworms, strip baits, salamanders, crayfish, or leeches.

Here, shrimp is added to a jig as an enticement.

- Offshore-trolling lures are frequently rigged with whole bait-fish, specially rigged to troll at relatively high speeds. Strip baits cut from the belly of a fish may be substituted.

Taste and smell attractants have become popular with some anglers. However, they are best used with lures that are fished slowly and deliberately, such as jigs and soft plastics. Attractants are seldom effective when used with trolled lures or lures that are cast and retrieved at high speed, since the scent dissipates too rapidly for a fish to find or follow the lure.

CHAPTER

Basic Lures and
How to Use Them

THERE IS AN ENORMOUS variety of lures, each designed to catch specific fish in particular situations. Here is a broad cross section of the many types of lures and their uses.

Surface plugs come in the chugger style (cupped face, makes a splash); cigar style (makes a wake but no splash); and cigar with propellers (make lots of bubbles and noise). Large and small sizes are available for both fresh water and salt water. Use them when you are fishing shallows, for any surface-feeding fish, or when fish are breaking the surface. A tip about buying these lures: Check the belly color, since this is what the fish mostly sees. Most are white, yellow, or black. Use white for bright days, yellow for overcast days, and black for dull days or night fishing.

Some saltwater surface lures actually sink. Their heavy weight helps you cast them on stout tackle, and also creates a wake and noise on your retrieve; the slanted face combined with a fast retrieve keeps them on or near the surface. They are fished by casting to schools of fish that are breaking the surface, or in areas where you suspect the fish to be close to the top.

Floating-diving plugs and crankbaits are similar—since you cast them out and reel (or crank) them back in. The former group may be designed to always stay on the surface, or they may dip down when retrieved quickly. Both can be used for trolling in fresh and salt water, but usually crankbaits are more popular for this purpose. Crankbaits can be designed as shallow, medium, and deep runners. The longer the lip and the closer it is to parallel with the lure body, the deeper the plug will run.

Topwater plugs are similar for both freshwater and saltwater fishing. These freshwater plugs include (top to bottom rows) wobble-type lures, chuggers or poppers, propeller baits, and plain stick baits.

Floating-diving crankbaits can vary in body shape, lip length, and lip position.

Long lips will cause crankbaits to dive deep; short lips will cause crankbaits to run shallow. Here, a variety of lip styles is shown.

The best lures to troll offshore from a large boat are skipping lures—large skirted lures designed to skip and bounce across the surface. Usually made of vinyl, wood, metal, and hard plastic, many are also brightly colored and sport large eyes to look like baitfish. The head of the lure has a center hole through which a heavy wire or monofilament leader runs; this is then cinched or snelled to a large ocean hook.

Skipping lures are primarily used offshore, but smaller versions are used inshore for coastal species such as bluefish, dolphinfish, and striped bass. The lures are trolled skipping on the surface, usually in the first or second wave behind the boat. You can use several designs or colors, fishing each from a different rod. With outriggers extended from the side of the boat, you can troll as many as eight lures at the same time.

Jigs and bucktails can be bare and plain to hold a soft plastic grub or worm, or they can be dressed with hair, synthetics, or feather tails. Replaceable rubber or plastic skirts are also popular in both fresh and salt water. Often tipped with bait or a soft plastic trailer, jigs are available in sizes ranging from $\frac{1}{80}$ ounce through 20 ounces. Most freshwater jigs weigh from about ⅟₃₂ ounce through ½ ounce; most saltwater, from ¼ ounce through several ounces. They can be cast or trolled (there are specific designs for each use), fished close to the surface, or dropped straight down to catch bottom fish.

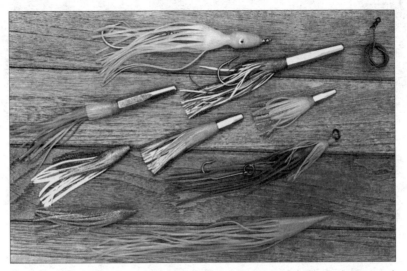

Vinyl trolling lures are designed mostly for saltwater fishing, and are made so that the line or leader runs through the lure before a hook is tied on.

In saltwater fishing, jigs can be used for deep jigging (as over structure or wrecks), casting, or trolling.

Structure spoons are thick metal lures used in deep jigging over reefs in salt water, surf casting along coasts, and deep fishing over structure in fresh water. Many styles, sizes, and finishes are available, but most tend to be bright and flashy, and to employ treble hooks. The addition of a swivel to this rig will often prevent the line from twisting as a result of the spoon's action in the water.

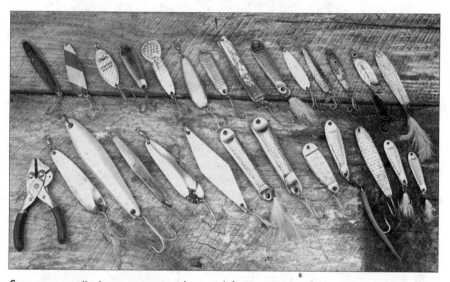

Structure or jigging spoons can be used for casting or for vertical jigging, since they are heavily weighted and will sink rapidly.

Casting spoons are curved to make them wobble when trolled or retrieved. Often they are fished around weeds, so they require a wire weedguard. Casting spoons with free-swinging hooks are used mostly in salt water; those with a fixed hook, more often in fresh water.

Trolling spoons are much like casting spoons, but are generally larger. Some use a single hook fastened to the spoon; others have a free-swinging single or treble hook. To take them deeper, trolling spoons are sometimes rigged with an in-line or drop sinker.

Spinners have a central shaft with a rotating blade that flashes and attracts fish. They are primarily used for casting and retrieving in fresh water. Sizes to catch everything from trout to muskies are available, in many styles, finishes, and colors. Spinners tend to twist line, so a good swivel is essential.

Casting spoons are often made in weedless styles (as shown in these examples), for fishing in weeds for bass, pike, and walleyes.

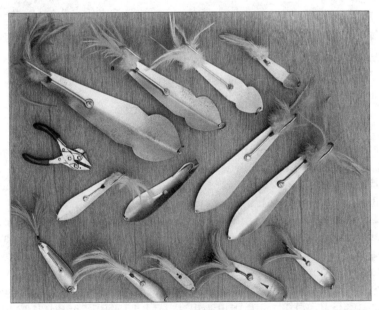

Trolling spoons are used in open water, and thus seldom have weedguards. Since they are made of thin metal and designed for a lot of wobble in the water, they are difficult to cast.

Spinners are among the most popular of lures for all freshwater fishing, since many styles are available for everything from trout to muskies.

Spinnerbaits look like jigs, but have a safety-pin-like arm that extends from the leadhead. At its end are one or two blades that rotate and flash; a skirt just behind the head covers the hook. Spinnerbaits are designed for freshwater fishing at a variety of depths, but primarily for bass and walleyes using weight-forward spinnerbaits.

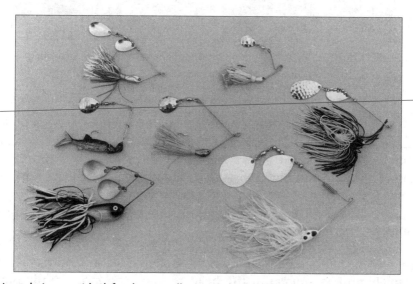

Spinnerbaits are ideal for bass, walleyes, and pike. They are worked under the surface.

Buzzbaits slightly resemble spinnerbaits, but use a wire form bent in a J shape. One or two propeller blades are then attached onto the end of the short upper arm of the J. As with spinnerbaits, a skirt covers the head. Buzzbaits are most effective when worked on the surface for bass.

Buzzbaits can come in safety-pin-arm or straight styles, but all are designed to be worked on the surface, where the blades churn the water and attract fish

Soft plastics comprise a large arsenal of lures for fresh and salt water. Many are close imitations of natural baits, such as worms, crayfish, lizards, slugs, shrimp, or baitfish. Others resemble nothing in nature and rely on their color, shape, and action (from arms, skirts, or other features) to attract fish. Soft plastics may be trolled, cast, deep-jigged, and fished in a wide variety of other ways for all freshwater and saltwater fish.

Trolling skirts are usually made of thin vinyl cut into slits. They are rigged with a leader through the body of the lure and a weight (usually an egg sinker) in the head to keep the lure skipping and swimming properly. They are also used as an additional skirt attractant in front of a trolled baitfish or strip bait. You can fish trolling skirts on the surface or deep by adjusting the trolling speed and/or sinker weight.

Tube lures are like small trolling skirts with a short skirt section. They are generally made in smaller sizes for freshwater fishing and rigged like plastic worms. Larger sizes are also available for saltwater fishing.

Fishing Methods: Shore, Boat, and Wading

THERE ARE MANY methods of catching fish, each with its own advantages and disadvantages. Shore fishing, for example, is relatively easy and inexpensive because you don't need a boat, and it can be done in most fresh water and salt water, from piers, jetties, and bridges. Wading allows greater access to good fishing holes, but it must be practiced safely. In contrast, fishing boats are nothing more than platforms that allow access to areas you could not otherwise reach. They are essential for getting quick and easy access to a wide variety of fishing spots on any water.

To fish effectively from shore, you need to study the water to determine where fish are most likely to be found. Here are some tips to make your shore fishing more productive.

- Focus your efforts on places that you are reasonably sure are frequented by fish, such as near drop-offs, brush piles, rocky formations, areas of standing timber, and weed beds.
- Places that offer easy road access or parking are often heavily fished by shore anglers. Instead of fishing these spots, spend time locating more productive areas farther afield. Often these will provide better fishing, since they will be less crowded, and the fish will be less wary.
- When bait fishing, try using a rod support. This can be a simple forked stick stuck into the ground, a commercial rod holder for the same purpose, a rod holder clamped to a folding chair, or a sand spike stuck into the sand or soft ground. For surf fishing, use a stronger store-bought sand spike.

Flipping or swinging a bait from the end of a long rod is an effective way to fish the edges or weed beds, such as this one in Florida.

Surf fishermen often use bait to attract fish that are in the sloughs and off the bars of beaches, and use hollow tubular spikes to hold their rods.

- Remember to adjust your tackle to the particular type of shore fishing that you are doing. Around rocks or off a jetty, use a long rod that will help keep your lures or baits from snagging on the rocks as you retrieve them.
- If you are pier or bridge fishing high above the water and directly over the fish, use a short, stout rod for more leverage in retrieving lures and fish. Also consider using a bridge net or gaff to help land the fish. A bridge net consists of a weighted net frame, supported at three points around the perimeter, that is lowered by rope to net the fish. A bridge gaff is simply a large treble hook on a rope, dropped to sink under the fish, which is then hooked as with a regular gaff. Some commercial piers have these devices available.
- When you are walking around a shoreline using lures, as in pond fishing, it helps to move in the direction that keeps your rod hand closest to the water. Thus, a right-handed fisherman would move clockwise (to the left) when fishing spinning tackle (held in the right hand), and counterclockwise (to the right) when fishing bait-casting tackle (held in the left hand).
- Chumming, or spreading baits to attract fish, can be a useful strategy. This often works best when you spread chum a day or two in advance. Good bets include doughballs, kernel corn, ground beef, prepared commercial baits, and ground chicken livers. Some types of chum, such as kernel corn and chopped chicken livers, work best if molded into a shell casing of bread or dough so the bait will stay together as a ball until it disperses in the water. Try to keep all your throws in the same general area, and cast your baits to the same spots the next day.
- If regulations allow, you can chum by tossing insects or baits to individual fish. Fly fishers sometimes do this with crickets, beetles, grasshoppers, ants, and similar terrestrial insects to see if there are fish holding in pools—and what they are eating.

Wading allows more versatility than shore fishing, but it requires caution and careful preparation. Check with local authorities for information on safe wading areas. These can vary with the seasons or local conditions, such as hydroelectric releases or ice-up, so use due caution. Here are some tips for safe and effective wading.

A right-handed spin caster should work clockwise around a pond, since it is easier to work parallel to the shoreline this way.

- Remember that rivers and streams can vary widely in depth and current velocity between dry and rainy periods. The area you waded safely during low water might be a dangerous raging torrent after a storm.
- Always use the right wading gear. In all but the smallest streams this means a personal flotation device (PFD). Many of these are made as comfortable fishing vests, complete with pockets, for ease of wearing under any conditions.

- Wear the right shoes. They should have good ankle support and soles that grip the bottom. Soles may have rubber cleats, metal cleats, or felt. Metal cleats and felt are used most often for slippery, alga-covered rocks in trout streams. Rubber soles are best for muddy or sandy bottoms.
- Wade wet in summer, wearing lightweight long pants for protection against rocks or brush. (But don't forget to bring a change of clothes for a dry ride home after fishing.)
- Hip boots come up to the crotch; waders come to the chest or just under the arms. Although you can wear waders in deeper water, they can also get you in trouble. Always use a wading belt around the outside of the waders to prevent taking in water should you slip and fall.
- Remember to carry any valuables (wallet, car keys) in a zipper-lock bag. This is especially important when wet wading.
- If you are wading in deep water, use an over-the-shoulder pack or shorty vest to keep your lures and flies as high and dry as possible. If flies, lures, hooks, or tackle do get wet while wading, open all the boxes once you are home and dry them out thoroughly to prevent rust.
- When wading in unfamiliar water, test each step before committing your weight to it. Some coastal areas and many rivers have sharp drop-offs or sloping rocks that can get you into trouble. Consider using a wading staff, or pick up a stout stick along the streambank for additional support and probing.
- Remember to keep your body at a right angle (sideways) to the current to lessen water pressure. Make sure you are prepared if a fish should suddenly strike and throw you off balance.
- When wading in the surf, be sure to move periodically, since the tide and current tend to dig a hole around your feet, putting you lower in the water.
- When surf fishing while wearing waders, consider adding a waterproof parka over the waders to prevent water from coming in.
- Do not wade through good fishing areas. The purpose of wading is to get to spots that would be impossible to reach from shore. Practice fan casting (casting all around you) to search for fish before moving to a new spot.
- An ideal fishing method is to cast across a stream and let the lure or bait swing with the current, retrieving only after it is

straight downstream. Alternate casts can be straight upstream using a fast retrieve, or quartering upstream with a moderate retrieve.

Boats allow you to fish deep water or to get to spots that would be impossible to fish from shore or by wading. Many types of boats are available, including canoes, small plastic-molded pond craft for one or two persons, aluminum johnboats, V-hull boats of aluminum or fiberglass, specialized fiberglass bass or walleye boats, center-console boats for light-tackle shallow saltwater fishing, and bigger boats for trolling, deep jigging, and drifting. The ideal boat is big enough for the water, weather conditions, and number of people aboard, as well as having ample storage for tackle and gear.

Canoes and small prams are ideal for one or two people in gentle rivers, ponds, and small calm lakes. Bass boats are specialized craft with casting platforms, rod lockers, and high-performance engines to rapidly cover a lake. Walleye boats are designed with high sides for

Small aluminum johnboats like this are ideal for much freshwater fishing.

rough big-water lakes, and mounting facilities for downriggers and trolling. On ponds or quiet waters, some anglers use belly boats: inflatable doughnut-shaped devices with a center seat where you sit wearing waders. Flippers allow propulsion and steering.

Bass boats are expensive, but their large engines allow you to cross long distances rapidly and fish a variety of hot spots.

Here are some tips for boat fishing under a variety of conditions.

- Make sure to follow all safety guidelines, and to have all the boat and safety equipment required by federal, state, and local regulations. These rules occasionally change, so check for current information.
- Store all tackle so it is out of the way yet ready to use when you need it. If you have your own boat, consider rod and tackle holders and racks to make fishing easier.
- Trolling is an easy method of boat fishing that allows you to cover a lot of water and find fish in unfamiliar spots. For trolling,

however, you may need a small auxiliary engine. Trolling speeds are generally slower for freshwater than for saltwater fishing.

- Drift fishing from a boat with bait or lures works best with a slight tide (in salt water) or a current (fresh water). Drift fishing in rivers sometimes requires a drag anchor to slow the boat and hold the bow upstream. The best drag anchor for shallow waters is a yard-long length of sturdy chain tied to a short rope.

- Chumming from a boat involves dispensing ground-up bait that spreads with the current or tide to attract fish to your anchored or drifting boat. The secret of chumming is to attract fish without feeding them too much. Try placing the chum in a net bag or large bucket punched with holes, tying it to a cleat so that it rests in the water, and letting the rocking of the boat distribute the chum.

- Casting to a specific structure or target area from a boat demands proper boat positioning. In fresh water, trolling motors are sometimes mounted on a boat's bow to hold a position or move along a shoreline.

Chumming—as is being done here in salt water for stripers and bluefish—allows you to work from an anchored boat, attracting the fish to you.

- You can maneuver a boat manually to hold it in position, or to follow fish, by using paddles or oars; in shallow water, you can use a long boat pole to propel the boat.
- When you are casting from a small boat, make sure your casts are at a right angle to the length of the boat, to avoid hooking fellow anglers. For the same reason, use short rods and overhand casts, never sidearm casts.
- When fishing to breaking schools of fish, do not run the boat near or through the school; this will put them down. Instead, cut the engine upwind, upcurrent, or uptide, so you drift into the school as you cast lures or baits.
- Finally, when trolling for breaking schools of fish, troll in a concentric circle around the outside of the school; this will drag your trolled baits into the school without putting the fish down.

Where to Find Fish

I F YOU WERE to divide a body of water with grid lines, some squares would be very productive, others devoid of fish. Each species must have the right combination of food, water temperature, protection from predators, and clean, oxygenated water in which to live. Because these requirements vary for different species, you need to be able to identify the best fish habitats.

Fish can generally be divided into two groups: structure-related fish and temperature- or thermocline-oriented fish. Structure-related freshwater fish include bass, walleyes, sunfish, perch, crappies, catfish, carp, pike, and muskies. Saltwater structure-related species include striped bass, sea trout, croakers, spot, sea bass, grouper, bonefish, snook, and West Coast inshore species such as rockfish. All saltwater species, even if structure related, move about and migrate more than freshwater species.

Some fish are described as *anadromous*, because they are ocean fish that are caught primarily as they make spawning runs into coastal areas or up rivers. These include shad, steelhead, Atlantic salmon, and the many species of Pacific salmon.

Temperature-oriented species include freshwater fish such as lake trout and steelhead, as well as Pacific salmon stocked into the Great Lakes; and saltwater fish such as bluefish, dolphinfish, tarpon, and similar species. Techniques vary widely for each of these types of fish. For structure-related fish, there are a number of things you should be looking for in the water habitat. In fresh water, you must pay attention to wood: logjams, standing timber, downed timber, stumps, brush piles, beaver dams, and beaver houses. Fish also school around rock formations: rock piles, gravel bars, riprap, old foundations, gravelly points, boulders, rock shelves, and rock around bridge pilings.

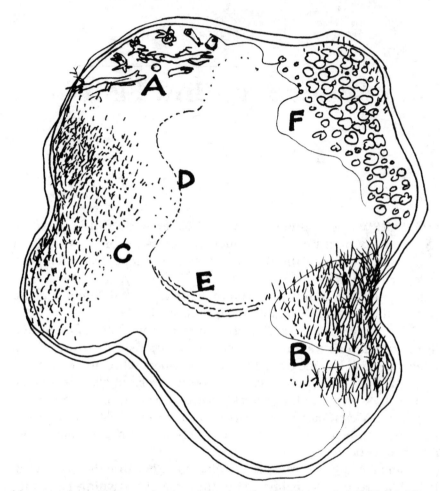

Most ponds and lakes and many rivers have typical spots that hold fish. These include: **A**—stumps and downed trees that hold bass and crappies; **B**—points and coves bordered by grassy beds that hold bass, pike, and carp; **C**—grassy flats that hold bass and pike; **D**—the edges of weedy flats; **E**—sharp drop-offs, called break lines, where fish hold and rest during the coldest winter months and the hottest summer days; and **F**—flats with thick lily pads and similar thick weeds.
Cliff Shelby

Weeds are an excellent source of protection for fish, and also an environment that breeds the small creatures on which they feed. Any type of surface weed (such as lily pads and spatterdock) or underwater weed (such as milfoil and coontail) is likely to hold fish. The edges of these areas are frequently the most productive.

Man-made structure in fresh water includes bridge pilings, piers, jetties, concrete walls, boathouses, docks, and duck blinds. Dams are often productive areas for migrating and feeding fish.

Typical structure in salt water can also include wood, although there is far less of the natural variety—other than southern mangrove and cypress, as well as some floating logs or stumps. In these waters, look for rocks in the form of cliffs, shorelines, and islands. Other natural homes for saltwater fish are coral heads and channels through coral reefs—both of which can be very productive. Weed beds and brackish water around weedy areas are both good holding areas for fish. On the West Coast, kelp beds are particularly productive. Man-made structure in salt water includes fishing piers, docks, bulkheads, channel markers, boathouses, bridge pilings and supports, jetties, inlets, buoys, and floating debris.

Fish gravitate to a specific type of structure because it offers food, shelter, and protection from predators. Knowing the fish's preferences can help you find the fish you seek. For instance, largemouth bass like wood, smallmouth bass like rocks, walleyes like gravel, and crappies like brush piles. Most saltwater fish relate to anything available—making rock jetties, concrete bulkheads, iron bridge piers, wood channel markers, and similar structures all good fishing spots.

Currents or tides can also determine where a fish is located in relation to a structure. Since structure helps provide protection against a strong current or tide, most fish will be on the downcurrent side, although a buffer ahead of this can also hold fish. In tidal situations, fish locations will change about every six-plus hours.

The sun also determines where fish hold near shallow structure, because fish often hide in the shade with their heads facing sun-lit water so that they can see and capture prey. Whenever possible, cast to shady sides of structure first. The shade will change, of course, on a long sunny day. A bright sun will also keep fish tight to structure, while fish tend to cruise or move away from structure on overcast days. Plan accordingly.

In thick underwater structure, use lures and rigs that are less likely to snag or catch. Jigs, soft-plastic worms rigged weedless, weedless spoons, and similar lures are best in these areas. The weedless hooks described earlier are made specifically to fish baits in thick structure.

Some saltwater fish hang out under floating debris. Dolphinfish are well known for this habit. If you encounter floating debris or planks offshore, troll around them or cast to them for any fish that might be holding underneath.

When you are boat fishing, you can usually see rapid changes in water depth in clear water, or determine them by a depthfinder. Fish are often plentiful in such areas, so take time to fish around sharp drop-offs or over shoals or shallow-water areas. These underwater hummocks hold both freshwater and saltwater fish.

In fresh water, temperature-oriented fish include primarily the trout and salmon species. In large lakes, these species do not relate to structure, but follow the temperature and oxygen gradients that form in any lake and are usually related to seasonal changes.

In summer, large bodies of water stratify, with a thin middle level separating the cold, deeper water from the shallower, warmer water. This thermocline layer often has the best combination of oxygen and temperature. Schools of baitfish are attracted to this level, making the thermocline perhaps the most productive spot to seek temperature-oriented gamefish.

The best technique for temperature-oriented fish is trolling, either conventionally or with downriggers. These sophisticated rigs have unique advantages for finding cruising fish; temperature gauges and oxygen gauges wired to surface readouts make it possible to put lures right on the thermocline at any depth you wish.

Since trolling in thermoclines is often deep trolling, bright lures in yellows and oranges are very popular, with spoons and neon-colored crankbaits catching many of the fish. Most anglers constantly experiment with subtle changes in colors and brightness.

Anadromous species such as Atlantic salmon, shad, and Pacific salmon begin their runs up coastal rivers based on light levels, water-temperature ranges, and other seasonal indicators. Within the same species, runs begin in warmer southern waters far earlier than in colder northern waters. For example, shad might begin their runs in Florida in December and January, in the mid-Atlantic area in April, and along the Northeast Coast in June. Be sure to pay attention to light factors as well. Many fish that make spawning runs seem to hit better during low light, such as on overcast days or during early-morning or late-evening hours.

Most species do not make a straight run up a river, but instead move back and forth several times in bays and estuaries before beginning a run. If you are fishing for salmon and shad, look for deep pools in rivers. These are good holding spots for anadromous fish, which rest in them between arduous spurts of running upstream past riffles and even waterfalls.

Tackle Use and Care

FISHING RODS, REELS, LINES, and lures are tools, and must be cared for as such if they are to perform properly year after year. Here are some valuable tips for taking care of rods.

- Store all rods straight, in a dry, clean area, so they will not take a bend or set. Special racks are made for this purpose, or you can make your own to store rods vertically or horizontally.

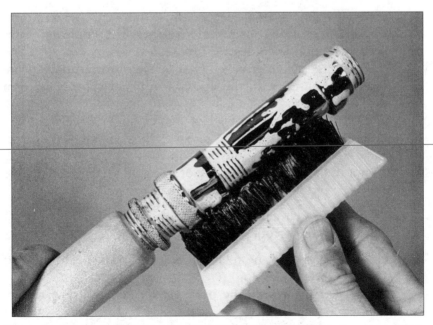

The best way to clean rods and reels is with a brush and sudsy water, scrubbing away dirt and salt (if saltwater fishing).

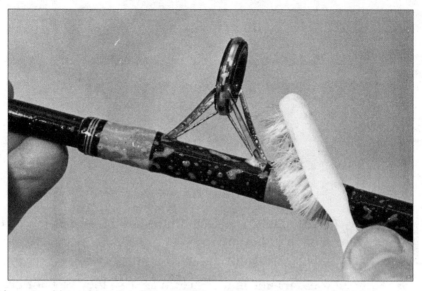

Here, an old toothbrush is being used to scrub around a guide frame.

- Wash rods after each use, especially if they have been in dirty or salt water. Use a brush or cloth to wash carefully and thoroughly around the guides and reel seats.
- To keep line guides from coming loose, restore rod-wrap finishes as required with the epoxy rod finishes available from most tackle shops.
- Do not use a rod for heavier or lighter lures or weights than recommended. The line- and lure-weight recommendations are listed just above the handle on most rods.
- Do not use a rod to push a lure or hook off a snag. Such in-line stress can often cause a rod to break or crack.

Reels need special care, because they have so many working parts that can rust or corrode.

- Spool the line onto the reel so it is firmly packed and filled to within ⅛ inch of the rim.
- Always use line within the pound-test range and type recommended for the reel.
- After fishing, back off the drag; otherwise it may become jerky or sticky the next time you use it.

- Wash each reel after use, particularly when fished in dirty or salt water. Scrubbing with warm water and a small brush is the best way to remove salt and dirt.
- After a reel is dry, spray it with a demoisturizing agent (such as WD-40 or CRC) to protect the metal parts.
- Periodically oil and grease each reel. The parts that need oil are the handle, rotor, and line roller in spinning reels; and the level-wind track and axle in casting reels. Add grease to the internal gearing and the levelwind worm gear in casting reels. Fly reels require little greasing—only on the gears, on the pawls, and around the handle. Most reel manuals will give you additional details on your tackle.

Fishing line gets worn and damaged with regular use. Here are some tips on proper maintenance.

- Pack line tightly on all reels. This will help prevent knots and tangles.
- Remove and replace all line once each year—more often if you fish frequently.
- Strip off any line that is abraded or damaged while fishing.
- Clean fly lines with a mild detergent or special line cleaner, then rinse and dry.
- Store fly lines in loose coils, or on the reel, provided that they are clean and dry.

Don't overlook lures and hooks, which also need regular attention.

- Check lures at all times for hook sharpness. Dull hooks are a prime cause of missed strikes.
- Remove and replace any broken, damaged, or rusted hooks. Most hooks on lures are easily replaced using split rings and split-ring pliers, available at tackle shops.
- To keep spoons and spinners shiny, polish them with a metal polish and then coat with a clear protective finish.
- Metal lures such as spinners, spoons, and jigs can be repainted during the off season.
- Store soft-plastic lures in separate bags sorted by color and type; otherwise the various colors will tend to bleed.
- Separate soft-plastic lures and hard baits in your tackle box; some of the soft baits will attack the finish on painted or hard-finish lures.

Finally, several tools are essential for the care and maintenance of fishing tackle.

- Keep pliers handy when fishing; they are ideal for unhooking fish, adjusting hooks, modifying lures, and taking care of a variety of other fishing emergencies.
- Always carry a hook hone or sharpener to sharpen hooks as you are fishing.

Bibliography

Dunaway, Vic. *Vic Dunaway's Complete Book of Baits, Rigs and Tackle.* Rev. ed. Miami, Fla.: Wickstrom Publishers, 1998. An excellent book on the subject, and invaluable for any angler.

Kugach, Gene. *Fishing Basics: The Complete Illustrated Guide.* Harrisburg, Penn.: Stackpole Books, 1993. A good overall book on all types of tackle, techniques, lures, baits, and fishing rigs.

McNally, Bob. *Fisherman's Knots, Fishing Rigs, and How to Use Them.* Jacksonville, Fla.: McNally Outdoor Productions, 1995. A good book with lots of knots, variations of rigs, and other connections.

Pfeiffer, C. Boyd. *Modern Tackle Craft.* Rev. ed. New York: The Lyons Press, 1993. An encyclopedic work on the making, modification, and care of all types of tackle, including lures and rigs.

_____. *The* Field & Stream *Tackle Care and Repair Handbook.* New York: The Lyons Press, 1999. Details the care and maintenance of all types of tackle, including rods, reels, lines, lures, tackle boxes, and accessories.

_____. *The Compleat Surfcaster.* New York: The Lyons Press, 1989. Complete coverage of surf-casting tackle and techniques.

Rowe, Barney. *Rigging Up Right to Catch More Salt Water Fish.* Ocean City, Md.: Ocean City Guide Service, 1983. Another excellent booklet in this series.

_____. *Catching More Flounder/Fluke.* Ocean City, Md.: Ocean City Guide Service, 1992. Specific details on catching these bottom fish.

_____. *Catching More Fresh Water Fish.* Ocean City, Md.: Ocean City Guide Service, 1993. A broad but useful book of tips on inland waters.

Sosin, Mark, and Lefty, Kreh. *Practical Fishing Knots.* New York: The Lyons Press, 1991. A good basic book with much information on all types of knots, splices, and connections for lines and rigs.

Soucie, Gary. *Hook, Line, and Sinker.* Rev. ed. New York: Holt, Rinehart & Winston, 1994. An excellent book with detailed information on all types of terminal tackle.

_____. *Soucie's Fishing Databook.* New York: Nick Lyons Books, 1985. An out-of-print but excellent book with complete information on swivels, snaps, lines, tackle, sinkers, hooks, and more.

Sternberg, Dick. *Fishing with Live Bait.* Minnetonka, Minn.: Cowles Creative Publishing, 1996. Excellent treatment and full-color photography of baits and rigs for freshwater fishing.

Walters, Keith. *Catching Striped Bass.* Bozman, Md.: Aerie House, 1993. A good basic book on catching striped bass using a variety of techniques.

Whitman, Lou. *The Complete Bait Angler's Guide.* Merrillville, Ind.: ICS Books, 1986. An out-of-print but informative book about baits—finding, caring for, and fishing them.

Index